Hell Gate Bridge

A Memoir of Motherhood, Madness, and Hope.

Barrie Miskin

Hell Gate Bridge

A Memoir of Motherhood, Madness, and Hope.

Barrie Miskin

woodhall press

Woodhall Press | Norwalk, CT

woodhall press

Woodhall Press, Norwalk, CT 06855
WoodhallPress.com

Cover design: LJ Mucci
Layout artist: LJ Mucci

Library of Congress Cataloging-in-Publication Data available

ISBN 978-1-960456-02-1   (paper: alk paper)
ISBN 978-1-960456-03-8   (electronic)

First Edition
Distributed by Independent Publishers Group
(800) 888-4741

Printed in the United States of America

This is a work of creative nonfiction. All of the events in this memoir are true to the best of the author's memory. Some names and identifying features have been changed to protect the identity of certain parties. The author in no way represents any company, corporation, or brand, mentioned herein.

For Patrick and Nora

Prologue

I've always been good at remembering names. I like to make people feel comfortable.

But during the first year of my daughter's life, I lost that gift. I even struggle to recall the name of our ob-gyn, the name attached to the hands that first gripped our baby as she entered the world. I recently had to ask my husband to remind me. All the doctors and specialists we were sent to see, most of them have blurred together in my mind.

The dates though, the dates I remember clearly. The date I arrived at the psych ER, the dates of the inpatient hospitalizations, the outpatient hospitalizations. The date of our baby's birth. The date when I looked at a photo of our family and saw that I had returned to myself and that we had returned to each other.

Four months before our daughter was born, December 4, 2017, that's the first date. That was the day I became lost.

———

By then I wasn't sleeping. I hadn't gone to work in a week. I lay down each night, tracing the pattern on our bedsheets until the design began to pulse, my hand on my belly, waiting for the baby's kicks. If they didn't come quick enough, I paced the apartment.

We had moved to Queens in July, but the corners of the rooms were still littered with unpacked boxes. They cast shadows on the slick wood floors, the streetlamps piercing the curtainless windows. My breath was quick and shallow as I slipped through the rooms. On each of my rounds, I'd pause in the kitchen and check the red clock hanging above the stove: 3:30, 4:30, 5:00. Retracing my steps to the bedroom, I listened for the first coos of the mourning doves announcing the passing of another sleepless night.

Patrick, my husband, slept on the couch at the suggestion of our new psychiatrist, another doctor whose name now escapes me. But he couldn't sleep, either. The doctor's rationale for our separation was so that I could cobble together a few hours of uninterrupted rest, but we had been cocooned together each night for nearly four years. It made us feel estranged.

———

When morning came, Patrick sat on the edge of our bed in a Hanes undershirt, pulling on black socks, getting ready for work while I begged him to stay home, even though I knew he couldn't. We had no other choice. I was an elementary school teacher and Patrick worked at a small art museum. We couldn't afford to both be home at the same time.

I knew that as soon as Patrick left, the fear would creep in again. Another blank day stretching before me like the hall in a house of mirrors. Everywhere I turned, everywhere I looked, there I was. What terrified me most were bridges. Queensboro, Triboro, Hell Gate—they called to me, inviting me into the gray, chopping currents of the East River beneath their long, hovering decks.

In that early December morning, facing the emptiness of our apartment and the day ahead, I tried to summon the wisdom of our new psychiatrist, cradling each of her suggested remedies like a precious talisman. *Do some yoga. Call a friend. Take a bath. Read a book. Make a cup of herbal tea.* Which of these mundane acts would be the key to unlocking the encroaching prison of my mind?

I decided to take a walk. There was a park, Astoria Park. Patrick and I went there once over the summer on one of my calmer days, packing bagels and watching the container ships pass. It would be my destination. I imagined picking up groceries from our shopping list at the C-Town on the way back, cooking a simple dinner, returning home renewed. The sleepless weeks behind me. The panic cooled.

That morning I chose to wrap myself in Patrick's clothes. An old green hoodie, scratchy woolen gloves from the army-navy store. I pulled out my Brooks running shoes, untouched since the previous spring, from under our entryway bench and zipped up a parka from the winter before that now hung off my frame. I was six months pregnant, but the anxiety thrumming through my body made me smaller than ever. I wound Patrick's blue flannel scarf around my neck and tucked my chin inside.

3

———

Outside, it was cold for early December, and I startled a bit at the bare trees and sharp wind as I walked west toward the park. The neighborhood was still unfamiliar to me, and I didn't like it. I missed our old neighborhood in Brooklyn, our friends, the cozy bar across the street from our apartment. Queens was too busy, too garish. Here, we lived across the street from a CVS.

I turned right, down Steinway Street. The fluorescent lights in the Payless and Edible Arrangements window displays felt unusually bright, and I stiffened as I passed by the old men smoking their cigarettes and sipping their coffees outside the hookah bars, sure of their disapproving stares.

As I crossed Astoria Boulevard and onto the pedestrian overpass above the freeway, the cars rushed east. I bargained with myself not to look down, tucking my head deeper into the scarf and quickening my step.

I reached the edge of the park, stopping to marvel at the joggers, their breath making neat puffs in the wintry air, at the mothers talking on their phones and pushing their babies. I felt a combination of envy and disbelief. How could they just carry on with their lives at a time like this? And then I realized, with a profound disappointment, that the emergency was only happening to me.

Testing myself, I walked quickly down the jogging path, a slice of blacktop cutting through a hill dusted with dead leaves, my sneakers tripping over the pavement as I descended. At the bottom of the hill, the path ended and I reached the river. My breath came in gasps, and I placed a protective hand on my belly, the other gripping the icy railing that only came up to my waist. Four feet of cold metal separating me from the East River. Hell Gate Bridge loomed above, its dark red arches wide open and menacing like a giant steel mouth, waiting to swallow me whole.

I had the sensation then of being zipped up inside a plastic bag, like the kind someone used to store an expensive suit. Everything dimmed as though a gauzy veil had been draped over my head, leaving me to view the world in a pale, ochre light. We'd been to this park before, but now it felt like I was visiting for the first time inside a fever dream.

I knew then there would be no groceries, no dinner at home, no getting through the expanse of the day alone. Hands shaking, I peeled off a woolen glove and fumbled for the phone in my purse.

"Babe." My voice was high and choked. "I need you to come get me. I'm in Astoria Park. I can't remember how to get home."

Chapter One

When Patrick and I decided we wanted to have a baby, I was thirty-eight years old: "advanced maternal age." The phrase terrified me. It made me think of systems shutting down, shriveling up, becoming defective. Advanced maternal age begins at thirty-five and I was already three years past the deadline, a distant bell toll that was growing louder.

I had been on a low dose of Zoloft since my early twenties for anxiety and depression. How much of the anxiety and depression was true illness and how much was circumstantial, I couldn't be sure. I stopped seeing a psychiatrist soon after I secured my first prescription. Psychiatrists were expensive, boring. Instead I got my refills every six months from a general practitioner in Williamsburg who could be found ponied up to the neighborhood bar on Bedford Avenue most weekdays by noon.

I suspected I should take myself off Zoloft when I was trying to get pregnant, but I never asked a psychiatrist. Instead I asked the general practitioner, who shrugged and said, "Sure." I was on a low dose, and it wouldn't be a problem.

I did my own research—reading article after article on the subject that terrified and shamed mothers into believing that antidepressant use directly correlated to autism in children. These were not articles I found on panicky mommy message boards or Facebook. These articles were in the *New York Times*, the *New Yorker*, published studies from Harvard.

I titrated myself off the medication throughout the spring of 2016, taking a smaller amount of the pill each week until I was licking specks of dust off my fingers by the beginning of May. I felt okay, I reasoned. That wasn't so bad.

Peeing on ovulation tests daily, I waited for the smiley face to let me know that it was time to have sex with Patrick, an act that was growing more and more utilitarian each time we got in bed together.

I've always been a little obsessive, but my all-consuming compulsion to control getting pregnant was out of character, even for an anxious person like me. The warning signs were there from the beginning, but we hadn't recognized them. How could we have known? On the morning in late May when the pink line appeared, I was already twisted deep in the knots of anxiety, and we had only been trying for a month.

Two days later, I got my period. I'd had a chemical pregnancy, an early loss of an unviable, fertilized egg. It would be unfair to compare the loss to a miscarriage, but the outsize grief I felt made it seem as though that was what I had experienced. I became more and more reclusive—a constant, queasy jitteriness running through me, like the moment just before a wet champagne glass slips through your fingers and shatters in the kitchen sink.

After the chemical pregnancy, my behavior grew strange. I was convinced that hairs and spots were appearing on my face and body, and I began checking for these illusory changes, waking up at 3:00 a.m to sneak into our tiny bathroom and examine my face in the mirror, tweezers in hand. In my mind, my body was growing dysfunctional, both internally and externally. A few stray hairs on my upper lip and chin—normal for me—became a thicket. A small beauty mark on my cheek was a drop of watercolor ink, blooming, multiplying by the second.

This warped obsession is classified in the *Diagnostic and Statistical Manual of Mental Disorders*, fifth edition (DSM-V), with other obsessive-compulsive disorders: body dysmorphic disorder. My body mutating through the smokescreen of my delusions. The beginning of my descent.

I was off from teaching for summer break, and I spent the days wandering around our Brooklyn neighborhood, alone. It was mid-June, and we were moving into our new home in Astoria, Queens, in a few weeks; but I was trying not to think about it, leaving most of the packing and cleaning to Patrick. The new apartment was much larger than our tiny one-bedroom in a fifth-floor walk-up, but I didn't know anyone in the area and was sad to leave our community and friends.

I started sneaking into the bathroom more and more while Patrick was sleeping, knowing that my behavior was strange enough to frighten him. Sometimes I spent over an hour in front of the mirror as I checked my face and neck, revolted by the sight of myself but unable to look away.

———

I had never been sneaky with Patrick, never withheld any information, never kept any secrets. Talking was our connection; it was how we built our world together.

When we first met in the summer of 2012, Patrick was subbing for the drummer in my best friend's band. I was off from teaching for the summer and spent my time riding my bike under the tree canopies during the humid, lazy days and going out to see my friends play music at night. I noticed Patrick right away; he was long and lanky behind the drum kit, his body loose yet in control. He wore white T-shirts and, behind his black heavy-framed glasses, his eyes were crystalline blue.

That whole summer, we sat on my fire escape and talked and kissed and smoked packs of cigarettes, lacing our fingers together until the busy Brooklyn street where I lived grew silent and the sky turned a deep navy just before the arrival of dawn.

Exhausted and happy, we'd lie down in the queen bed that took up most of my bedroom, the backs of our thighs imprinted with tiny diamonds from the metal landing of the fire escape, the cheap air conditioner humming loudly as we twisted ourselves up in the cool sheets.

I spent my twenties and thirties choosing men who added layer upon layer of wet concrete, cementing into place a low self-worth I never quite outgrew. The men I chose were too young, too old, too emotionally unavailable, too unwilling to leave their adolescence behind. There were bass players living on the dole, professional motorcycle racers, record store owners. Anyone who could make me feel like I wasn't cool enough or attractive enough to stand by their side. And the hurt from their inevitable yet swift rejections of me stung for months, sometimes years, longer than they should have.

Patrick was different. He was steady, uncomplicated. He made me feel like I could finally rest, like I could sit down and just breathe.

I brought Patrick back to my apartment for the first time after a Fourth of July party. It was so hot, the hottest night that summer. I wore short black cutoffs and blue tennis shoes, my hair piled as high off my neck as it could go. The party wound its way to a metal bar in Bushwick, Brooklyn. We shared a cigarette outside and I tugged gently on his T-shirt, pulling him toward me for our first kiss, crust punk kids waving sparklers all around us.

After the bar, we took our bikes back to Greenpoint on the subway, blasting ourselves with the freezing train car air.

We got off at the Bedford station, our necks and faces salty with dried sweat. The Avenue was quiet, punctuated with a shout or a laugh. As we walked down the empty street, Patrick steadied his bike with his right hand and gently slipped his left arm around my shoulders.

"You taking me home with you tonight?" he asked, shyly, teasing. I nodded, looking at the ground, demure and smug, my eyelashes touching the tops of my cheeks as I lowered my eyes and grinned without opening my mouth.

After that night, we never slept apart again. Not until the doctor suggested it.

Chapter Two

On July 1, 2016, we moved into the Queens apartment. It was huge, with a dining room, two nonworking fireplaces, and a room just off the bedroom that we would turn into a nursery. In the backyard, peach, pear, and cherry trees bore plump, edible fruit. And it was affordable. To this day, the apartment remains a New York real estate miracle, but I hated it. We didn't have enough furniture to fill the rooms, and the space felt vacant and cold. On our first night there, a roach scuttled across Patrick's pillow, startling him out of his sleep.

By mid-July, we learned that I was pregnant again, but I couldn't celebrate. By then it was too late—I had taken up residence within my mind, a place that was growing darker by the day, devoid of any joy. I didn't talk to anyone except Patrick and my parents that entire summer, but even with them, I felt like I was being hollow and dishonest. I wandered the rooms of our new, empty house, checking my face in every mirror.

Throughout the early months of my pregnancy, my obsession with my appearance grew. Fixing myself was an itch I couldn't scratch, no matter how deep I dug into my skin. I was desperate to alter the monster I believed I was morphing into on the outside so I could erase the demons that were taking up residence within.

I became consumed by beauty treatments. I bought $200 pigment correcting creams for the imaginary spots, traveled to Manhattan on weekends to high-end waxing and threading salons, and priced out Invisalign with receptionists at different dental offices for teeth I imagined were shifting in my skull. If I had to leave the house, I caked on foundation and wore sunglasses and a baseball cap. As soon as I got home, I sat on the counter in our bathroom, inspecting my face in the mirror above the bathroom sink for any new changes.

In the beginning, Patrick tried to chalk my behavior up to early pregnancy nerves and out-of-whack hormones. He humored me, pulling me into the bright light of our kitchen and snapping pictures of my face with his phone. He showed them to me. "See?" he'd say; "more beautiful than ever."

"You're wrong," I replied, pointing to an imagined darkened patch of skin. I pushed the phone away. "You see that? You're wrong."

———

When we went to the ob-gyn, I never asked questions about our baby's growth or birthing plans or healthy food or vitamins I should be taking. I only asked if these changes to my appearance were normal for pregnant women. Our doctor looked at Patrick, bewildered, and said, "I don't see anything. I'm not sure if your husband does." Patrick shook his head, his mouth set in a grim line.

By late November, the need to fix myself burned through me like liquid flame. I needed something quick, affordable; something that could give me any sense of relief. I made an appointment at an Astoria salon where the stylist spoke no English and I spoke no Greek. She had no idea what I wanted, and I couldn't communicate it to her, but I needed to dig, to find relief. I went forward with our visit. She slathered an eggplant-colored dye all over my head, staining my forehead and temples. And it burned.

I got what I deserved.

I was already a bad mom. Hair dye, creams, waxing. The two cups of coffee I had every morning that a friend offhandedly mentioned might have been the cause of my chemical pregnancy. Hadn't I read *What to Expect When You're Expecting?* I hadn't.

A mother was supposed to be gentle, natural, nurturing, careful. The embodiment of peace. The opposite of me.

The dye charred my scalp to the point where chunks of skin flaked off my head and onto my back and shoulders for weeks. The combination of pain and shame kept me awake through the night. I stopped sleeping, haunting the rooms of our house and dreaming of ways I could make myself disappear.

———

Patrick wanted me to see a psychiatrist and I agreed. By that time, I was existing solely within my dark thoughts, and he began to sense what I was too frightened to speak out loud.

We found the psychiatrist through Zocdoc. The week before Thanksgiving, it was nearly impossible to find a doctor who had any available appointments, but this doctor's time slots were wide open. She took our insurance. She had four stars and a professional-looking headshot. Her office faced Central Park West.

The psychiatrist only met with me in person once, but over the next six weeks, she spoke with me in fifteen-minute bursts over the phone, charging us for each call. She put me on Lexapro, Wellbutrin, tiny pink pills of Benadryl to help me sleep. We checked each medication with my ob-gyn and he okayed them, but I detected judgment in his tone. Nothing worked. Finally, the psychiatrist took me off Lexapro and put me back on Zoloft, rationalizing that if it had worked for me before, it would work again. But this time, it didn't. She raised the dose. And when it still didn't work, she raised it again. And with each new dosage, I heard the crescendo of madness grow louder inside my head.

Chapter Three

When we returned home from Astoria Park that early December morning, Patrick made me call the new psychiatrist right away. He stood so close that I could still feel the cold from his parka. The doctor answered and I tried to articulate my state, my words moving too quickly yet weighed down by my heavy tongue.

"Do you have racing thoughts?" she asked.

"Racing thoughts?"

"Yes, are your thoughts moving quickly? Are you having thoughts of harming yourself?" the psychiatrist paused, a heavy silence as she waited for my reply.

My father is a psychiatrist, so I had a solid understanding of the lingo. I realized what the doctor was trying to imply—that I was having a manic episode. That bipolar disorder was an option on the table.

I willed away the diagnosis. This was anxiety, a series of panic attacks. I had had this before; we just needed to find the right combination of medication that could soothe me and not cause any harm to the baby.

"No," I lied. "I'm not having any thoughts like that. I think it's the Zoloft you prescribed me. I think the dose is too high. I think we need to try a different medication."

"Listen," the doctor said, "I work at Kings County Hospital. I'll make sure you have a bed. I'll monitor you myself. The baby will be monitored. We can try different medications, see how you react. Get you sleeping. I just had a patient who told me she quite enjoyed the experience. There's a journaling workshop."

I knew nothing about psychiatric hospitalizations, but the way the doctor framed it, I had to admit, sounded vaguely appealing. I imagined myself covered in white blankets, warm socks on my feet. A monitor by my side where I could keep a constant vigil on the baby. Doctors bringing me different medications with water in waxy paper cups. I would rest. Finally sleep. I could journal about it in the morning.

"Let me ask my husband," I replied. "I'll call you right back."

But Patrick wouldn't let me go. Not yet.

—

Every day became more grueling than the last as my world tilted further askew on its axis. I grew to hate waking up in the morning in my newly alien body and mind. I opened my eyes at the start of each day, testing out the world to see if it had returned to normal. It never did.

I asked Patrick once during those weeks if he "remembered me." I wanted Patrick to reassure me that I was still the person who radiated joy, delighted in my friends, was teased for being such an easy laugh. I lay on our bed, crying when I asked him this. He just held me for a long time, rocking me steadily until my sobs quieted and I could finally fall into a fitful sleep.

Later that winter, when things had gotten so much worse than either of us could have imagined, I asked Patrick if he was going to leave me. "I feel like you already left me," he replied, defeated. "I feel like you left me a long time ago."

———

I had been looking forward to the holidays that year. My brother, his wife, and my two small nieces were flying in from Paris. The McIntyres were having their annual forty-person Christmas celebration at Patrick's Aunt Sally's sprawling countryside home in Pennsylvania. And I always got secretly excited about the drugstore gifts I received from my students—gold boxes of Ferrero Rocher chocolates, $10 Starbucks gift cards, ornate bottles of perfumed hand lotion, misspelled notes.

What I had most been looking forward to, though, was our one-year wedding anniversary, three days after Christmas. The year before, we had gotten married at Del Posto, a sumptuous Italian restaurant in downtown Manhattan. It was an intimate wedding, no more than thirty members of our friends and family. I walked down the aisle with my mom and dad by my side, floating into the room on the shimmering intro to "High" by the Cure.

We served fat steaks and pillowy ravioli stuffed with pumpkin and mascarpone, the glasses filled with champagne, scotch, and wine. In my favorite photograph from that night, Patrick and I sit next to each other at a dinner table full of flickering tea lights. Our eyes are locked on each other, dazed smiles on our faces. In the picture, I am still wearing my veil. I wouldn't take it off all night.

19

Months before the anniversary, I ordered my dress for the occasion. It was black crushed velvet with a high neck and an open back. I would wear it with purple suede platform pumps and black tights. I imagined pointing to my bump and telling the waitstaff proudly that we had just gotten married in the same spot one year before. Look at us now!

By the time our anniversary arrived, I no longer wanted to celebrate. I had spent the December weeks not working, and I was becoming scared to leave the house. I lay on the nubby brown couch in our living room, trying to focus on some HBO TV series or *Seinfeld*. Mostly I stared at the white walls, grappling with why our living room was steadily becoming more menacing, creeping into my new, unfamiliar world.

I've always been in charge of holidays and decorating our apartment. Patrick still retains his decorating sensibilities from his bachelor days in Brooklyn. But that winter, he went and bought a small tree on his own, adorning it with white lights and ornaments that he found at CVS. During those hours on the couch, I had a hard time looking at it. The voice that thudded in my head repeated, "You don't deserve this; you don't deserve this." The tree just reminded me of the time I had once looked forward to so much but now couldn't bring me any joy.

I called the psychiatrist every few days, panicking. Eventually she went to Europe to celebrate the holidays with her family. She answered my call once while she was there. She charged me for her time and never answered again.

We never got to celebrate with my brother and his family. We never made it to Aunt Sally's. But we did end up going to Del Posto for our anniversary. I wore the velvet dress and Patrick wore his wedding suit. We posted a picture of ourselves dressed up on the way to the restaurant on Instagram with a cheerful caption: *Anniversary dinner for three!* I look pretty in the picture. My bangs are dark and sleek, and I have a wide, flushed smile. If you look closely, though, you can see that I am frightened. My pupils are dilated, and the smile is tight.

At the restaurant, I struggled to remain normal. We talked about music, friends, our wedding the year before. I still pointed out my belly to the waitstaff, and our server had the bartender make me elaborate mocktails. Patrick ordered the Chef's Tasting Menu. Our bill ended up being outrageously expensive.

Before we stood up from the table, Patrick leaned over and whispered in my ear while smoothing the back of my hair.

"You're so beautiful, honey," he said, his voice thick with sadness. "I'd marry you again. I'd marry you again right now."

Exhausted from feigning normalcy, I asked Patrick if we could take a taxi back to Queens. In the cab, I gripped his hand and shut my eyes, frightened by the speeding blur of city lights outside the window.

Chapter Four

Ever since the psychiatrist suggested I might need to be hospitalized, I became obsessed with the idea. In my mind at the time, the hospital was where people who were sick went to rest and recover, and I needed to do both for me, for Patrick, for the baby.

I concocted a fantasy that if I were to admit myself to the hospital, my condition would not be treated as a mental illness but as a pregnancy-related one.

Patrick worked on the weekends then, and I spent those days alone poring over message boards, collecting stories of women who had suffered from peripartum mental illnesses, desperately trying to connect with anyone whose experience mirrored mine. In my searches, I found a few stories of women who had suffered from suicidal ideation while pregnant and had received treatment at hospitals. Their stories always ended with gratitude for the doctors who cared for them, and deep connections with the patients they intimately shared with in group therapy sessions. They would return home healed and serene, left to revel in the bliss of the remaining months of pregnancy, their sleepless nights and dark webs of thoughts behind them.

Mommy message boards are extremely popular in the United Kingdom, and what I failed to realize as I was reading these reassuring tales is that all these happy endings were written by women living in the UK. In the United Kingdom, pregnant women suffering from mental illnesses are treated very differently than their American counterparts. There are psychiatric hospitals that are designed specifically for the care of women suffering from peripartum and postpartum mental illnesses. Every single staff member in these hospitals—doctors, nurses, social workers, physician's assistants, even receptionists—are highly trained to specifically treat maternal psychiatric disorders.

In these specialized hospitals, women are treated in the same space as other pregnant mothers, or mothers who are suffering from postpartum illnesses. The mothers who are suffering from postpartum disorders have their babies at their side to encourage the bonding that might not take place had the mother been separated from her baby.

My internet searching hadn't gone deep enough, though, because what I failed to discover was that this care for peripartum, postpartum, or truly any kind of mental illness does not exist in the United States. Here, I quickly learned, if you are mentally ill, you will be treated like a criminal, pregnant or not.

Inside my increasingly unreliable mind, I fantasized that once admitted to the hospital, I would be taken directly to the Labor and Delivery ward, where I would be monitored and provided with sleep medication that had been vetted by trained ob-gyns as safe for the baby. There, I would rest, be fed nourishing meals. Patrick, doctors, and nurses an arm's length away through the day and night. I dreamed of the other pregnant women who would be there. We would share with one another, creating a bond that would last through the birth of our babies.

I never imagined a psych ER. I never imagined being locked in a psych ward. I never imagined the shaming and cruelty and mistrust. I never imagined being alone.

———

On January 3, 2017, the holiday break ended, and I went back to work. I expected to be better by then, but there had been no reversal of my condition, no relief. Each day, I felt zipped up tighter and tighter inside the plastic bag, so tight I could barely breathe.

Getting ready for work that day, I carefully chose a dress I had bought for Christmas Eve and never got to wear. It had an intricate floral print and kimono sleeves with a sash that tied right above my belly. I blew my hair dry and drew a cat eye on my lids. It was more important to me than anything, then and for years to come, that no one could tell that there was anything wrong with me, that no one could tell how dark and sick I had become inside. As far as my friends and co-workers knew, I had suffered from a bout of panic attacks and was on the road to feeling better. In a way, I was also desperate to hide my sickness from myself, convinced that if I made myself look normal, I would feel normal; if I made myself act like everything was fine, then everything was, indeed, just fine.

At work, people passed me in the halls and told me I looked beautiful. I was quiet that day, mostly out of fear, and pasted a serene, closed-mouthed smile on my face, adding to my beatific glow. I did a simple project with my class where the students wrote down their New Year's resolutions, earnest promises to be nicer to their sister, to eat the vegetables their mom served them at dinner.

At 4:00 p.m. I clocked out and walked home. It was still getting dark early, and with the setting sun came the reminder that I was closing in on another sleepless night. Patrick came home from work and cooked a pasta dinner. I was calm as we spoke about our days. If I act normal, I will be normal.

We watched a few episodes of *Seinfeld* and I changed into my pajamas, taking a Benadryl before getting in bed. It must have been around 9:00 or 9:30. I drifted off for a bit and then woke about an hour later—10:30 on my iPhone. From the moment I picked up my phone from the night table, I knew sleep had eluded me once again. I sat on the edge of the bed, put my head in my hands, covered my face, and screamed, savage and raw.

Patrick came over to sit next to me and put his arms around me, but I shook him off. I got up and started digging through the laundry bag.

"What the hell are you doing?" he asked.

"I'm packing a bag. We're going to the hospital. I need to sleep. I need to sleep for the baby . . . my not sleeping is hurting the baby." I was crying, hard. The words came out in choked gasps.

"I'm not having my pregnant wife, my wife and my baby, staying in a mental hospital. I'm not."

"It's not going a mental hospital! They'll take me to Labor and Delivery. They'll get me sleeping. I need help . . . I need someone to help me . . . please!" I was having trouble catching my breath. "Please," I said, gulping for air. "Please."

Patrick touched his forehead and shook his head, breathing hard as he turned away from me and walked out of the bedroom.

We went back and forth all night. I paced quickly through the apartment, always pacing, then I wrapped myself in Patrick's green hoodie again, pulling the arms of the sweatshirt tightly around my body like a makeshift straitjacket, my breathing hollow. Each time I entered the kitchen, the red clock on the wall taunted me, the black numbers shouting each passing hour that I was awake when I should have been in bed, nourishing my baby with peaceful sleep.

Patrick tried to calm me down, tried to hold me, make me breathe, massage my shoulders, my legs, my feet. I pushed him off me each time. I couldn't be still.

He grew tired and frustrated, walking into the living room to take breaks from my hoarse sobs, trying to make sense of what I was begging him to do. Then he returned to me, tried to steady me. He searched my face, desperate to find me, terrified when he saw I was no longer there. That I was already gone.

My pleading continued until dawn. By the time morning broke on January 4, Patrick, exhausted and bewildered, finally relented.

Chapter Five

We climbed up the steps of the 57th Street Station and out into the unseasonably warm January morning. The sun was dim in the shadow of midtown office buildings, and people walked purposefully on their way to work. Patrick and I held hands the whole way from the station to the entrance of the Emergency Room, but we didn't speak.

Upon entering the sliding automatic doors, we found the waiting room of the ER oddly quiet. A lone man rocked in a plastic chair, cradling his hand wrapped in a crimson-soaked towel. Besides him and the security guard picking distractedly at a rhinestone on her manicure, we were alone.

At the security desk, the guard lazily looked up from her nails. "ID," she drawled. We handed over my driver's license, my insurance card. She wrote down my name on a list and slid the cards back across the desk without looking back up. "Go have a seat," she said. We chose chairs as far away as possible from the man with the injured hand, like he was a bad omen. Patrick placed his hand protectively over my knee and I threaded my fingers through his as we waited.

Ten minutes passed and an intake nurse emerged from a small office in the corner of the waiting room. She was round and full in her navy scrubs and flipped her long braids over a shoulder with a wave of her hand. "Miskin," she called, glancing at her clipboard. Patrick and I both rose. "Just her," said the nurse, pointing at me. I looked over at Patrick, hesitating. He jutted his head toward the nurse, silently telling me it was okay. We didn't realize then that this was the first of many times we would be forced to separate in the coming months.

"This will only take a few minutes," the nurse said; "a standard intake." I thought I heard pity creep into her voice as she sensed our fear. She would be firm yet warm, a combination unique to New York City nurses. I could trust her.

———

We sat down in the small office, surrounded by laminated security glass windows. All business, she checked my heart, my eyes, took my blood pressure; asked me how far along I was.

"Twenty-seven weeks," I said. Again, I noticed my voice becoming hesitant and childlike. I still wore my winter coat, unzipped, and I reached down instinctively to touch my belly.

She clicked her pen and looked directly at me, the pitying warmth returning to her face.

"So," she said, "what's been going on?"

I told the story, the one I would tell countless times for the next year to nurses, doctors, residents, medical students, social workers. I couldn't sleep. I was scared for the baby. The baby needed me to sleep. My husband needed me to sleep. Was there, by any chance, some medication, some magic pill that could just make this disappear?

30

Could someone just help me get some rest, get some peace, please?
If I could get just one good night's sleep, this might all go away.

The nurse didn't take her eyes off me, nodding as I spoke.

She lowered her voice. "Are you having thoughts of hurting yourself?"

The nurse's chin nearly touched her chest, her eyes raised, locked
on my face.

"Well, just like thoughts, I guess. I mean, I would never do anything
of course." I laughed nervously, my hand fluttering again over my belly.

"Do you have a plan?" she asked.

"No, nothing like that." The nervous laugh escaped again. "I mean,
I'm pregnant."

My mind flashed to the December morning in Astoria Park. Just
an icy, waist-high railing separating the East River and me.

The nurse held my gaze, steady, and I looked down at my lap, my
face burning with shame.

"Just thoughts," I repeated.

"Are you googling?" she asked. "Ways to do it?" She nodded gently,
like whatever I had been thinking, whatever I had been doing, it was
okay to share with her.

"I've been reading about other moms who tried it. To see what
they did. To see how they got help. I've been googling the number
for the Suicide Hotline. But I read that they can track your number
or send the police over ..." I trailed off. "Please," I whispered; "I just
need some sleep."

"Okay," she said slowly, drawing out the word. "We're going to get
someone to come talk to you. Get you checked out."

Then she picked up the phone, all business again, the warmth in
her voice suddenly gone. I wondered if I had imagined it. She turned
her head away.

"We've got a woman, thirty-eight years old, twenty-seven weeks
pregnant," she said in a low tone. Her voice dropped another

register. "She's thinking about," she paused, "she's thinking about," she whispered, "suicide."

Time began to move differently after that. Picking up breathless speed and then slowing down to interminable waiting. After the nurse hung up the phone, things moved quickly.

She opened the door of the tiny office and back into the waiting room, where a security guard stood. He was in full uniform: gun, baton, cuffs. It took me a moment to register that he was there because of me.

Patrick jogged across the room toward me, his eyes wide beneath his black-framed glasses.

"Take her bag," the guard barked at Patrick. "You'll need to stay out here. You can't come in the psych ER. Patient privacy." Patrick's mouth opened in pained shock. He couldn't summon the words quick enough to respond.

Behind the guard was a heavy door with a small window, glass crosshatching, like a door leading to the boiler room in a horror movie. The floor dropped out from under me and I began to exit my body, as though watching from a vantage point on the ceiling.

Here were the realizations that struck me: I was going behind the door. This was not the regular ER. Patrick would not be coming with me. I was being punished.

I had the same sensation—sinking dread—that used to come over me when I had brought home a bad grade in chemistry or got caught smoking in the parking lot freshman year of high school. I was about to get in trouble. But what had I done wrong? I was unwell, I was pregnant, I was terrified, and I was about to get taught a harsh lesson—about to get a talking to, about to be exiled from my husband, about to be locked away because of my thoughts? The absurdity, the unfairness, the pain in this moment of understanding lodged inside me like a cold, steel weight. It remains with me still.

"But my wallet, my insurance card," I stammered. "My phone; please let me keep my phone. If I need to talk to my husband, my family."

The security guard softened for a moment as he noted my bell: small, round, and firm beneath the stretched, striped fabric of my favorite maternity top.

"All right," he said, gruff and resigned. "Keep your phone."

He went to hold my arm, to lead me through the door, but changed his mind at the last minute and, with a hand barely touching beneath my shoulder blades, pushed me forward. I braced myself, focusing my gaze so intently on the heavy blue door that I forgot to look back at Patrick.

———

The door clicked shut behind me, and I sensed time slow again. A petite and soft-spoken psychiatric aide guided me to a bench. I sat, willing to give myself over to anyone who seemed like they might take care of me. "Did you have breakfast yet?" she asked, touching my shoulder.

I shook my head.

"Let's see if we can get you something to eat."

She left me alone and I took in my surroundings. The waiting room was small and quiet. Phones rang and people behind closed doors answered them in hushed voices. Everything was pale institutional blue, cold cinder blocks, a white-tiled floor.

The aide returned with a full tray and placed it on the bench beside me.

"Eat," she urged. "For the baby."

The tray was loaded up: pancakes, little rectangular packets of maple syrup, two small orange juices with foil tops that I had to puncture with a tiny straw, a mini bagel and a packet of grape jelly.

Pale pineapple cubes in a clear cup. There was a plastic fork and spoon but no knife.

I devoured the breakfast. All day, I ate sweets to make the baby kick—her movement proof I hadn't harmed her yet.

I pulled out my cracked iPhone that the guard had let me keep as his small kindness and texted Patrick.

They brought me breakfast on a tray! Pancakes with maple syrup. Surprisingly delicious!

I had a compulsion then to turn the horror of being hospitalized while seven months pregnant into a story that could be recounted as a tragic yet vaguely glamorous footnote. In the tabloids that week, I had read about Kanye's own psychiatric emergency in Los Angeles. This made me feel better about my situation. For months, even years, after the psych ward, I obsessively collected stories of celebrities who had undergone emergency psychiatric treatment, reassuring myself that I was in good company.

A vision floated through my mind of returning to work in a few days, belly protruding and proud, holding court during the daily lunch hour with my favorite co-workers. I would be brave and beautiful. A survivor.

Texting Patrick about being served breakfast on a tray would end up being one of my many attempts at rewriting the story. I wasn't being hospitalized for losing my mind; like the many celebrities before me, I was being hospitalized for exhaustion.

As I scraped the last of the grape jelly onto my bagel with the plastic spoon, a door to one of the offices opened and a man in his early thirties stepped out, crossing the short hallway to where I sat on the bench. I was struck by how young he was. With his full beard and thin, wire-rimmed glasses, he looked like he could be a bass player in a low-key shoegaze band, just a guy passing through the hallways of Patrick's practice space in our old neighborhood.

He introduced himself as the social work intern and asked me to repeat the story I had told to the intake nurse. He took out his legal pad and scribbled notes, glancing up every few moments and nodding, locking eyes with me, practicing his active listening skills.

Although I must have internally recognized that it was a lost cause with the social work intern, I continued to put my faith fully in every person I told my story to, gripping onto the hope that they would be the one to provide me with the clarity I so desperately sought.

The intern continued his scribbling and meaningful nods as another man strode purposefully over to our small huddle, a look of studied concern on his face. He too had a beard, although his was trimmed more closely. He wore a plaid shirt beneath his sweater, his sleeves rolled to his elbows to reveal heavily tattooed forearms. He offered me a warm, dry hand to shake and told me with authority that he was the psychiatry resident. I was again to repeat my story.

I began to gather that everyone in emergency psychiatric care was young—either an intern or a resident, still learning, blossoming into their new careers. The experts would come later, for those who were lucky enough to afford them.

As I continued to subtly erase my sense of self through the repetition of my story, I heard myself say phrases like "This isn't really our wheelhouse," or "This wasn't our usual jam," as though the psych ER was a dive bar we had unexpectedly dropped into for a last beer on our way home from a party.

I spent so much of my life, my childhood, my teens, my young adulthood with a simple yet sharp yearning to be pretty and cool. That is to say, I cared a lot about what people thought of me. I'm more quiet about it now, but I still do.

Even at age thirty-eight, twenty-seven weeks pregnant, voluntarily admitting myself to a psychiatric ward, I still wanted the approval of the bearded social work intern; I needed assurance that the tattoo-sleeved resident knew I was just like him.

After the nodding and note taking, the social work intern and resident conferred privately and then returned to me, letting me know that they now planned to meet with Patrick out in the waiting room. I had the inane thought that they would probably get along, recognizing themselves in Patrick's own rolled-up plaid shirt sleeves, hipster eyeglasses, and arm tattoos. Patrick would set them straight, reassure them that this was just a simple matter of readjusting my medication, that we could thank everyone for their time, head back home with the magic prescription in hand, and forget about the whole morning.

The resident pointed me to a small room, everything in shades of antiseptic blue and wan, mint green. In the room there was a low cot covered in white sheets, a small pillow at the head.

"Try and rest," the resident said and nodded in the direction of the bed. There was a window on the wall next to the cot. I took off my ankle boots, lay back on the small pillow, and looked up at a slice of blank sky between the tops of the office buildings. Inside me, the baby quickly flipped.

As the morning wore on, more patients cycled through, some wailing, some manhandled by the security guard in their resistance. When the social work intern and resident came back from their interview with Patrick, I decided I would let them know I was ready to go home. This was when I still thought I had choices.

———

Time slowed and I was alone. Maybe two hours passed. Less or more, I can't be sure. I still had my phone to check, but it was on a table across the room, and I was having trouble uncurling myself from the fetal position I lay in on the cot.

Each time I tried to lie down and sleep, dark memories pounded through my head like heavy drumbeats. Thud: *A cruel remark about my weight from an elementary school classmate.* Thud: *My dad pounding a fist on the dinner table, veins popping at his temples.* "*You lazy good for nothing.*" Thud: *Blackout drunk and sobbing uncontrollably at a party where most people were strangers.* Thud: *Stop being so anxious! It's not good for the baby!* Thud: *The East River. Hell Gate Bridge.*

It must have been early afternoon when the door finally opened. The intern, the resident, and a woman with a green sweater dress, long hair, and wooden earrings entered my small room. She was matter-of-fact, earthy; offering me a small, soft hand; introducing herself as the head psychiatrist on call.

"We had a chance to speak with your husband in the waiting room," the doctor began. "He's pretty frightened. He says you're not sleeping, that you're pacing the house. He says that you've expressed thoughts of hurting yourself. That he's found you searching for ways to do it on Google." She held my gaze. "Would you say that's true?" I looked down, nodded.

"We think it would be best for you to stay at the hospital, where you can be monitored for a few days. We don't have a bed for you here, but we do have one Uptown. How does that sound to you?" Even through my terror, the word "bed" still gave me a sickly sense of relief.

"Okay," I whispered, looking at the floor. "Can I speak with my husband?" I didn't look up, shame another weight on my already heavy head.

———

Against protocol, they let Patrick into my room in the back of the psych ER. He sat with me on the low cot, arms wrapped around my waist as we skimmed papers and signed away our dignity with a ballpoint pen provided by the social work intern. Patrick appeared steady, solid. He would keep up that appearance for the next six months, until the pain and anger of the experience would seep through and subtly reshape him.

The intern placated our fears with soothing answers to our frantic questions: *Of course the hospitalization is voluntary. Strongly recommended, but voluntary. She can leave any time she is ready. I'm sure she won't be there more than two days. Yes, they will monitor the baby; they will monitor Barrie, make sure any drugs prescribed are working. Yes, she will rest, she will sleep, she will be taken good care of. Her and the baby.* None of this ended up being true.

———

For years to come, I had a notion that there was a jumble of strings inside my head, like the embroidery floss you might find discarded in the bottom of a sewing tin. If I could just pull out the correct thread, I would be able to unravel the knot of my insanity. In the early months, I played a lot of magical thinking games: If I hadn't made this decision . . . If I had told the doctor something different . . .

The thread that held the decision to make Patrick bring me to the Emergency Room that January morning ended up being a thread I pulled out of the tangle and examined often.

———

I spent all day on the cot in the psych ER, the hours of the day passing by without me. It was nearly midnight by the time the stretcher was rolled outside the door to my little room, waiting to strap me in and wheel me into the ambulance that would bring me Uptown.

Chapter Six

There were no lights in the ambulance, no sirens. The ride was smooth. We must have hit a green light on every block. I watched my belly rise and fall, covered by white blankets and protruding between two belts that held me onto the stretcher.

The EMT called back to me from the driver's seat. "You okay back there? Not too bumpy?"

"No, it's fine," I said in my new whisper voice.

"Good, good. Just want to make sure, a woman in your condition and all."

"I'm okay," I replied.

"So, what's the matter?" he asked. "Why am I taking a nice lady like you Uptown?"

"Just anxious. Depressed, I think. I can't sleep."

"Ah, you don't need to go to the hospital. If it was me, I'd be upstate at my grandmother's house. Fresh air. Have her feed me bowls of vanilla ice cream. Convalesce," he said, drawing out the "s." "You'll be out soon though. A good girl like you with a baby. They'll let you go soon. God bless."

I smiled, but we were facing away from each other and he couldn't see me. I didn't yet know what he meant by "They'll let you go soon." Who would let me go? Wouldn't I leave tomorrow? After a doctor had helped me?

We rode the rest of the way in silence, quiet when he lowered my stretcher out of the ambulance and rolled through the low-lit, carpeted lobby, quiet in the elevator that brought me upstairs to the ward.

The EMT punched a keypad outside the metal doors and they swung open. I was wheeled quickly down a hallway—too bright, too loud—until I was outside the glass-encased reception desk.

He gave me a half wave and turned around. Behind me I heard a sizzling buzz, visceral and electric, followed by a final, loud click. The heavy doors shut for the night.

———

A stout woman in green scrubs unbuckled me from the stretcher.

"Follow me," she said, bored. Her white sneakers squeaked on the cold, waxed floor. She held her clipboard in front of her purposefully, but her shoulders were rounded with exhaustion. I followed her, sliding in my socks. My shoes had somehow disappeared and I had been put in huge pajamas made of blue paper. They kept slipping off my hips and down my shoulders.

"I'm pregnant," I called after her.

"We know," she said, her voice flat, not turning around.

She brought me into an empty closet-sized room and shut the wooden door, turning on fluorescent lights that flickered dimly above our heads.

"Strip for me," she said, robotic.

"But I'm pregnant," I reminded her.

"You said that already. Strip, please."

I let the blue paper pants fall to the ground and slipped the top over my head. I stood before her in my underpants and bra.

"Take off the bra."

My hands fumbled with the clasp, and the bra dropped to the floor. She patted down my naked torso, dipping her hands under my heavy breasts, fake nails scratching my skin.

"Okay," she said, yawning, "your belongings are at the front desk. Your shoes, your jewelry, your phone—screen's cracked, by the way. You'll get them back when you get out. Any questions?"

"Is my baby going to be okay?"

She took her eyes off her clipboard and looked up at me.

"People have had babies in worse situations than you. Jail, concentration camps. Your baby will be fine," she said, her voice still devoid of any emotion.

She had just stripped me, humiliated me, dismissed me, but still, I held onto those words for a long time. It was the most comforting thing I had heard all day. I looked down at my finger. They had somehow missed my wedding band. I tapped it compulsively during the next four days, a Morse code to remind myself that I was once normal and that I was still loved.

———

The nurse led me to a small wooden table and pointed to a low plastic chair.

"Just sit here and wait," she instructed.

"I haven't eaten since breakfast, is there anything I can have?" I asked.

After a few minutes, an orderly dumped a tray of cold hamburger and applesauce in front of me, clattering to the table. I still ate, hoping for the baby's kicks, for a signal, but she was quiet and still.

I sat. I waited. My body felt grainy with exhaustion and fear. A young man walked toward me. Like the nurse, he looked purposeful but tired. He couldn't have been older than twenty-five and introduced himself as the intern. "I'm just on rotation," he said, like he couldn't wait to get away from the mentally ill patients he had to deal with for the next few months, imagining himself landing a position as a heart surgeon or a dermatologist.

He asked the same questions as the interns in the psych ER, but unlike them he was removed and cold. He couldn't even bring himself to pretend to be warm or concerned or kind. He had a sparse mustache, and it made him appear pubescent. Under the thin line of hair, his lips wound into a sneer. He was disgusted by me. How could I have gotten myself into this mess?

"I think I've made a mistake," I told him once he was done checking the boxes on his questionnaire. "I want to go home."

His sneer deepened. "You want to go home? You see a judge."

"A judge?" I asked. I couldn't take in a full breath.

He put his palms flat on the table. "You were just in the ER telling them you were contemplating suicide. Seventy-two hours in here at least. You want to leave, we take you to court; you tell the judge why you're here, and he'll send you right back. Then you'll probably have to stay even longer."

"I thought this was voluntary," I said, my voice thin and high. "The doctors in the ER said . . . my husband and I understood this was voluntary. Please. I didn't do anything wrong; I just want help."

"Did you sign the papers in the ER?" he asked.

I nodded.

"You should have read them more carefully then." He glanced at his watch. "It's Wednesday night, so you'll have to stay longer than seventy-two hours. That's my guess. Doctors are off on the weekends, so the earliest we can release you is Monday. If that."

The nauseating buzz and click of the locked ward door sounded again. Mercifully, miraculously, Patrick arrived. I didn't think I would see him again. He introduced himself to the intern, shook his hand.

"She's going to be here until Monday," the intern told him with a solemn nod. "Visiting hours tomorrow at eleven and five." He got up and left Patrick and me alone, scraping his chair against the cold floor as he walked away.

There was nothing we could do, no one we could call to help. Patrick just held me as I wept into his jacket.

While I sat crying into Patrick's coat, a patient suddenly lunged at me, drool sopping the corners of her mouth.

"I love you!" she screamed, her face inches away from mine. "I love you! Please, please help me. You have to get me out of here. Help me!"

I covered my eyes with both hands, shielding myself from her like a bad dream. "Please," I whispered. "Don't."

I learned she had postpartum psychosis. That she had a one-month-old daughter at home. I found a picture of her discarded inside a book in the ward's library cart, a picture of her dancing with her husband on their wedding day, her head thrown back and her mouth open in joy. Her face was almost unrecognizable. Her husband had brought it to her to remind her of how happy she once was.

The orderly who had brought me the hamburger came back and asked Patrick to leave.

"Closed for the night!" he told us, punching a fist into the air.

As soon as Patrick left, I ran to the phones to call him, a row of cream-colored landlines fixed to the wall.

I punched the numbers but kept getting the operator: *If you'd like to make a call, please hang up and try again.*

"Phones are closed, miss," the orderly told me.

"How do I make a call when they open?"

"The number from out of state?"

Patrick's number had a Pennsylvania area code.

"Yeah," I said.

"Then you're gonna need a calling card. If you know anyone in-state, you can call them free of charge." He jumped up to shoot an imaginary basketball.

A nurse appeared then, small and older. She had glasses on a lanyard around her neck.

"Let's get you to your room," she told me.

The room was carpeted and larger than I had expected. There were two beds, one already occupied by a woman with a long, dark ponytail.

"Towels are here," she whispered, pointing to a low shelf. "And you can sleep here," she said, gesturing to a wooden twin bed. Above the bed was a whiteboard with the word "Joy" scrawled in green marker. I thought this was a reminder of how I was supposed to be feeling. The nurse saw me noticing. "That's me," she said. "They post the name of the nurse on duty." She gave me a small smile and left me alone.

I tried to lie down but couldn't, so I got up to pace the halls. Joy gently caught my arm and gave me a Benadryl. "Imagine lying next to your handsome husband," she said. "Try to sleep."

I finally lay down. I had taken so much Benadryl over the last month that it no longer had any effect. My roommate snored deeply on the bed across the room. I hadn't met her yet, but I hated her, feeling that she was mocking me by sleeping so soundly.

The door to our room remained open as aides walked by on a loop, checking on me, making ticks on a clipboard. There was a clock on the wall in the hallway, and I could see it from my bed. I watched the black hands turn and turn until dawn.

Chapter Seven

At 6:30 the fluorescent lights in the hallway came on and the ward slowly flickered to life. Across the room, my roommate continued to snore. I crept out from under my covers and into our shared bathroom.

In the reflective plastic slab that served as a mirror, my eyes were ringed with a black mix of cried-out makeup and a month of no sleep. The bad Queens dye job had made my normally straight, dark hair an unnatural auburn frizz. With trembling fingers, I twisted it into a stubby braid. My pupils were black and bottomless, the green irises around them thin. I looked scared and scary and strange. In my face, it was clear any light that ever existed in me had gone out.

I stripped off my paper uniform quickly and folded it as best I could, tucking it into a corner where I hoped it wouldn't be hit by the shower stream. Behind a moldy plastic curtain, the water ran weak and cold. From a dispenser on the shower wall, I pumped bitter antibacterial soap into my hand and rubbed it quickly over my body. I stopped for a moment to press gently on my belly. No sign of movement.

Shivering, I turned off the water and pushed the curtain aside. Hanging on a hook, I found a rough towel the size of a large washcloth and used it in an attempt to dry myself. As I dabbed at my wet skin, the door to the bathroom opened. All doors on the ward are rigged to remain unlocked. I was on Q20 observation, which meant I needed to be checked on every twenty minutes throughout the day and night.

Without saying a word, a nurse looked down at my naked body and back up again to catch my eye. She ticked her clipboard and turned around, disappearing into the morning.

Until the phones turned on at 8:00, I resumed pacing. Frantically padding the halls in my dirty socks, I had a chance to take in the lay of the ward, which was simple and small. At the center was a large, glass-encased nurses' station. From that point were two long hallways leading in opposite directions—one toward more bedrooms, the other to a dayroom with a cracked leather couch facing a small TV and VCR.

My pacing was interrupted a few times for a check of my vitals or a blood draw (the bruises that continued to bloom on my arms from these daily indignities serving as shame souvenirs that took weeks to fade), but other than that, I was mostly ignored.

As I moved through the ward, I checked out the other patients. In private, selfish moments, I was envious of those who suffered from brutal yet easily diagnosed afflictions: bipolar disorder, schizoaffective disorder, major depressive disorder. These were known; their names secured a firm place in our collective vernacular. I falsely believed that medication could help these patients be set back on track, to continue on the path of their day-to-day lives.

The patients who slept all day, who dropped their heads into their breakfast trays, knocked out with drug cocktails shot into their arms, who walked the thin line between existence and death, inspired a fierce and self-indulgent jealousy in me. I wanted to be lost to the world too. They seemed so free.

I knew with a quiet certainty that if I just had anxiety and depression, the Zoloft would be working by now. There was something more sinister happening in my brain, and I was too afraid to find out what it really was.

I had stopped being able to recognize my own image in the mirror, and as the days wore on, the world around me continued becoming more and more unfamiliar too. I had a new habit of touching simple objects—couches, tables, televisions—checking to make sure they were still solid and real.

Midmorning, the energy on the floor shifted as the team filed into the ward, chatting with one another, making plans for their day, holding water bottles and cups of coffee, dressed in suits or dresses with flats. We were ignored. Eyes straight ahead, the team reconfigured into a single line as they filed into an office. Over the silence in the room, we all heard the office door shut behind the final team member with a perfunctory click.

———

My parents had a New York area code, so I wouldn't need a calling card to reach them. Patrick had already been in touch with my mom and dad. They knew I was hospitalized but hadn't yet heard it directly from me.

Unlike Patrick's unwavering composure, which would eventually reveal its hairline cracks, my parents' moods and reactions changed jarringly, depending on the day. Each time we spoke, I didn't know what to expect. The roulette wheel spun from panic to blame to deflection to warmth to selflessness. Still, they picked up the phone every single time I called, and that morning, I really wanted to hear my mom's voice.

My mom had a difficult time talking about my illness. She still does. During those early years, she treated my sickness as an inconvenience. Later, when I was better and we were able to reflect on it, she would change the subject quickly.

That first morning on the ward, when my mom answered the phone, I could tell immediately that the roulette wheel had landed on inconvenience and blame. My parents knew I wasn't doing well, but Patrick and I hadn't been open with how sick I really was. Mostly, we didn't want to admit it to ourselves.

My brother, Zach, his wife, Celine, and my two nieces were in town for the holidays, and my parents had taken them to a hotel upstate for a few days while I was back in the city, checking myself in to a psych ward. Patrick and I hadn't been invited. I was supposed to be back at work.

"Mommy," I said into the phone, hot tears pooling into the receiver. "Mommy, I'm in the hospital."

"I know," she said, quiet and careful. "Patrick told me. What made you decide to do that?"

"I haven't slept, Mom. I can't sleep. I'm scared."

"That was a big decision, to check yourself in. Did you think it through?"

"I don't know, Mom. I just wanted help. Do you think it was a bad idea? That I won't get help here?"

"You're a married woman now, sweetie," she said. "You make your own choices with your husband. This has nothing to do with what Daddy and I think. This is between you and Patrick." She paused, the line silent.

"You know Zach and Celine are hearing back to Paris tomorrow. You're going to miss saying goodbye to him and the girls."

"I know," I said, shame flooding my throat.

"Have you felt the baby kick?"

"Not really," I said.

"Hm," she sighed. "Daddy and I will be there tomorrow. Call if anything."

We said "I love you" and hung up.

———

The hours between the phone call and Patrick's visit that first morning are mostly blank. I paced the halls or sat on the edge of the cracked leather couch in the dayroom, wrapped in a blanket and shaking from the combination of lack of heating on the ward and fear. There were old tabloid magazines laying around the rec room—usually a delicious guilty pleasure. I'd pick one up and flip through the pages quickly with my clammy, trembling fingers. I couldn't read anymore, unable to process the words. Anything that ever brought me pleasure had abandoned me.

Shortly before Patrick's visit, a fellow patient stopped mid-pace. He held out both his hands with palms open, a stop sign. "Miss, Miss!" he flipped his hands, pumping them downward. "You gotta slow down. Don't be so anxious. Here," he stage-whispered; "it's not good for the baby." He was probably around my height, wiry, smooth cheeked and wide eyed. He somehow managed to look almost hip with his paper pajama bottoms slung low, and he had the palpable charisma of a wisecracking cartoon sidekick.

"You remind me of my mother" (he pronounced it "MUTH-ah"). "She was always anxious. My aunt told me my mother was anxious when she was pregnant with me too. And see! Look what happened to me!" He presented himself holding his arms out wide, a sideways grin punctuated with a dimple. I couldn't help but give him a small smile back.

49

His name was Daniel. He was twenty-one years old. He lived nearby and worked at a Chipotle. He had spent the last year actively campaigning for Bernie Sanders. Daniel had a few female admirers, and they brought him take-out containers of Chinese food or bags of candy during visiting hours. His mother had just died after a long battle with cancer. He was in the hospital because he had fainted at work upon hearing the news, his legs buckling under him from the weight of his grief.

I have forgotten the names of most people I encountered on my journey into the world of mental illness. Trauma has a way of blurring the memories that cause you pain. But there were some people along the way who demonstrated small kindnesses, who radiated empathy, who had lessons to share. Who let me know they could still see me. Those people's names, I remember. Daniel was the first person whose name I remember from that winter. I still think of him, sometimes.

When the hands on the hallway clock neared 11:00, I rushed to the nurses' station.

Visiting that morning were my ward roommate's husband and her son, an impeccably made-up admirer of Daniel's, the family of the patient suffering from postpartum psychosis, dressed in traditional Orthodox Jewish clothing, and just a few others. Most patients on the floor spent visiting hours in their beds, alone. At the back of the group was Patrick, in a large green parka, black woolen beanie on his head.

There was no chance for us to run up and embrace our loved ones, though. Even with a small group, the procedure to enter the ward was painfully slow. Each visitor had to relinquish their phone to a guard behind the glass partition separating the nurses' station from the patients and their families. Then, one by one, they were patted down.

Most families had brought food, changes of clothing, books and magazines. Some brought reminders of home—framed photographs or stuffed animals. Each gift was examined, searched for drugs or cigarettes or tweezers, dental floss, or shoelaces. Anything we might be able to use to hurt ourselves or another patient.

I suspected the nurses liked to search the packages not only as a safety measure but also as a way to judge us. I'm sure it was nothing more sinister than that they were bored, and a few minutes of gossip about the patients gave them something to do. But for me, it was another addition to the growing list of humiliations as they pulled out the designer maternity jeans, copies of the *New Yorker*, and lace briefs that Patrick had packed for me, smirking knowingly at one another as they held up each item of clothing, examined it, and then shoved it, crumpled, back into the bag. I knew what they were thinking: *Here comes the pregnant spoiled brat.*

Patrick and I were finally face-to-face. We held each other close, our palms pressed to each other's cheeks. My whole body leaned into his as we walked down the hallway, as if I couldn't go on without him holding me up.

On the cracked leather couch in the dayroom, Patrick sat close to me and wrapped me in his parka. He had brought my favorite "healthy" pregnancy cravings: a spinach salad with grilled chicken, walnuts, and Craisins; an orange juice; a vanilla yogurt parfait with granola and strawberries. I ate it all quickly, hoping for movement from the baby. No luck.

I was often described by both my parents and Patrick during that time as "catatonic." I don't think they were wrong. I robotically repeated the same questions, voiced the same fears. Patrick and my parents gave me reasonable answers that I grasped for an instant but, just as quickly, slipped away. And I'd ride the loop again. Which is what I did as I sat on the couch in the dayroom that morning with Patrick during those first visiting hours.

I knew Patrick hadn't slept either. I knew he was exhausted from the subway rides to and from the hospital, the interviews with doctors, the horror of not knowing when his wife and baby would return home to sleep by his side. I knew that besides his parents and sister, he didn't have anyone to talk to. But I had zero capacity for acknowledging his suffering then. In my memory of the time in the psych ward, Patrick is just quiet and solid and steady, a body to lean up against, a jacket to cry into. He spoke to doctors, our friends, our parents, our bosses, the insurance company, but I never thought to ask him what they had talked about or if he and all the people we loved were okay. I only continued riding the loop that ran through my mind.

Chapter Eight

Before Patrick left that first morning on the ward, a tall doctor wearing a slim suit and red tie came over to the cracked couch where we sat and introduced himself, ducking his head a little as he offered us a warm, dry hand. He was older than the doctors who had met with us so far, closer to mine and Patrick's age than to college.

"Dr. Abrams," he said, shaking firmly, looking both me and Patrick in the eye. "So, I see we have a situation here," he said, smiling and tilting his head. With the other doctors, this would have come across as harsh and judgmental, but Dr. Abrams had a mild-mannered way about him. I liked his voice.

We told the story again. Dr. Abrams nodded, held our gaze.

"We're going to meet with you after visiting hours," he said looking at me, then Patrick. "We're going to get you better. Get you home." He shook our hands again, and Patrick squeezed my knee with relief. Finally, we thought, someone we could trust.

———

Visiting hours ended at 1:30 p.m. and then opened back up again at 5:00. Filling the time between Patrick's visits was agonizing, and meetings with doctors and social workers ended up taking place long after they had originally been promised.

After Patrick left, I changed into the clothes he had brought—clean underwear and socks, stretchy jeans, and a soft maternity top with tiny pink and blue flowers. I walked back into the dayroom and was met with a few open-mouthed stares. Now out of my shapeless paper pajamas, everyone could see I was pregnant.

I've never been in prison, but I am assuming the conversation among inmates is akin to the conversation among patients in psychiatric hospitals. It revolves around two questions: "What are you in for?" and "When are you getting out?" For the patients in the dayroom who were lucid enough to care, my fate became an object of fascination.

My roommate, now awake, kept coming over to put her hand on my belly. She brought me paper cup after paper cup. "Cold water," she murmured. "Good for the baby. Drink." Then she turned to the group. "She's my roommate!" she announced proudly to whomever was in the rec room. "The pregnant girl is my roommate!"

"You told us five times already. You wanna shut up?" yelled a woman with fuchsia hair and no front teeth from where she lay on the couch, legs splayed open.

But my roommate didn't shut up. She continued bringing me cold water and making her announcement with each cup. She was a mother too. Her son came during visiting hours. He must have been eleven or twelve years old. He looked frightened.

I wanted to connect with the other patients on the ward—to answer their questions, to ask my own—but I physically could not. My fear was actually choking me, the tight strings wrapped around my neck, making my voice come out in strange and tiny whispered breaths.

And I couldn't sit still. I wound tight figure eights around the ward, sitting on the couch for a few minutes in the dayroom; passing the wall of phones, touching each one as I went; loitering in front of the nurses' station; examining my hollow face in the plastic bathroom mirror; then circling back to the dayroom couch. And repeat.

———

Also similar to prison, the way out of a psych ward is through good behavior. As adept as I am with social cues and making good impressions, for much of that first day, I didn't realize there was a game to be played and that I was already making mistakes.

When Daniel had told me earlier to slow down, he wasn't doing so as a simple kindness. He had also wanted to let me know that I needed to clue in to the game. That we were being watched. That if I wanted to get out of there, I had better start behaving. And I did. I wanted to get out of there so much that my body trembled with adrenaline, preparing me for an escape from danger.

———

Later, when I began to fanatically research everything I could about mental illness, spiraling downward through Google searches, scholarly research from the National Institute of Health, the DSM-V, I discovered the mistakes I had made on the ward. My first mistake was not sleeping. The nurses' ticks on their clipboard throughout

55

the night revealed every time they had looked in my room and seen my open eyes staring at the ceiling—a sign that a patient could be in the throes of a manic episode. My second mistake was the pacing—psychomotor agitation. Again, signaling mania. Each time I sped by the nurses' station, a pencil scratched out another tick.

I started approaching anyone on the floor wearing a uniform to tell them through my choked whisper that I hadn't felt the baby move, that I had been told in the ER that the baby would be monitored, and would it be possible to get a sonogram? "Please," I would gasp. "I'm so scared. They told me they'd help me. Why won't anyone help me?" This was my biggest mistake. Repetitive questioning patterns are a strong indication of a thought disorder, and I was showing my hand, revealing that my thoughts were veering toward delusional. Another pencil scratch on the clipboard.

———

The hallway clock hands crept toward 3:00, and I still hadn't been seen by Dr. Abrams and the team. I had been on the ward for nearly eighteen hours, and no one had monitored me or the baby or really provided any help or comfort at all. We passed the time being herded to and from activities: music appreciation, arts and crafts, chair yoga.

In art class that afternoon, I spent an hour stringing plastic beads on an elastic thread in a class led by a young woman with a shiny, dark ponytail and a chunky diamond on her left ring finger. She had to cut the thread for me, since patients weren't allowed to use scissors. With shaking hands, I tied the ends together and gave the bracelet to my roommate.

At the close of class, we shuffled single file out of the art studio. Back in the dayroom, Dr. Abrams finally returned my eye contact, and a sensation of queasy gratitude overcame me. The team would see me now.

In the office where they had been sequestered since early morning, the team sat around a large wooden conference table with bottles of water, pens, and scrawled-upon notepads strewn before them. Anytime I saw people doing something normal—a workday meeting, for example—I seized with jealousy. That should be me.

I thought about Daniel's warnings. Being watched. As I entered the conference room, I pasted on my schoolteacher smile. I curled my shaking fingers inward so no one could see them. I pushed through the whisper voice.

I wanted to charm them. When the team asked if I was still having suicidal ideations, I made them laugh by telling them, "Nope! I'm scared straight!" I earned frowns and concerned head shakes when I recounted the false promises of the psych ER staff.

I left the meeting with a prescription for two different sleeping pills safe to take during pregnancy, an appointment with a nurse to check the baby's heartbeat before bedtime, and a promise for a private session with Dr. Abrams the next day to discuss my release from the hospital.

"Tomorrow, the work begins!" Dr. Abrams exclaimed, jovial. He clapped his hands, rubbing his palms together.

———

When we were together that evening, Patrick tried to help me relax by pretending it was just a normal night among friends. He spent the visit chatting with Daniel about Bernie Sanders. I ate my spinach salad with chicken and Craisins. We played a game of chess. Patrick and I planned for my first day home: We would see the new *Star Wars* movie in the theater and go out to eat afterward.

Cheeseburgers and a vanilla milkshake. Patrick told me I was going to sleep well that night. He promised that he would too.

———

Later that evening, I called my brother and his wife to say good-bye before their trip back to Paris. Celine had suffered from severe postpartum depression after the birth of her first daughter, my niece Zoe, and she would provide me with a great deal of comfort throughout my illness. She told me that after Zoe's birth, she had wanted to be hospitalized too, that there was nothing to be ashamed of. She reassured me that I had made the right choice.

Hospitalization for pregnancy-related psychiatric disorders would have been a very different experience for Celine, though. A mother living in Paris who suffered from a maternal postpartum disorder would receive treatment in a Mother Baby Unit. Celine would have had Zoe by her side while she was treated by a caring and highly trained staff. She would have had the treatment I had imagined for myself.

Instead, the patient suffering from postpartum psychosis on my ward was told by the nurses to "stop acting so crazy" or else she wouldn't get to go home to her one-month-old baby. She was dosed with so much medication that, on my last day at the hospital, I could see her lying in her room hooked up to a machine monitoring her heart rate, her head lolling to one side on her pillow.

———

I spent the rest of the evening sitting beside Daniel while he watched a football game on the small TV. Between us, we shared a brown paper bag filled with Sour Patch Kids delivered by one of his admirers. They stuck to my back teeth and sweetly puckered my mouth, coating my tongue with pure sugar. About ten candies in, I finally felt the baby kick.

As promised, Joy, my nurse from the night before, came and showed me how to listen to the baby's heartbeat through her stethoscope—a low-tech sonogram. Still, I could hear my daughter's heartbeat clear and steady and strong.

An orderly brought my sleeping pills—Ambien and Rozerem. The combination of these two pills was safe to take during pregnancy and much stronger than Benadryl, but this was the first time they had been offered to me. I swallowed them like I was receiving a benediction, changed into leggings and a T-shirt, and lay down. By 10:00, I fell into a black and dreamless sleep.

———

It was dark and silent on the ward when my eyes opened. The hallway clock read "1:30." The sleeping pills hadn't worked. Sometimes when patients have become overly agitated, they will "break through" their medication, rendering the effects moot. This is what had happened to me. I spent the rest of the night peering through my eyelashes like a child playing pretend as the nurses continued their rounds, marking checks on their clipboards.

———

Both my parents were coming for visiting hours that morning. While my mother reacts to difficult situations by becoming dismissive or avoidant, my father reacts by becoming mean.

Growing up, my dad could be cruel. Over the years, he has expressed deep regret for the way he treated me, and we have worked to build a relationship throughout my adulthood, but I wouldn't say we are close. If he answers the phone, I can't chat for more than a minute before asking him to put my mother on; if we end up alone together, we struggle for things to say. Still, I know he is trying, that he is proud of me. He's a good grandpa. And I do feel lucky we are able to have a second chance with our relationship. But sometimes I look at my daughter and try to fathom how an adult could have found it within themselves to want to hurt their little girl.

After the daily vitals check and blood draw and the filthy, cold shower, I dressed and found my mom and dad already sitting at a small table in the dayroom—true to form, with a huge bag emblazoned with the Zabars logo filled with bagels and crumb cake. I was a little embarrassed at how out of place they seemed, with their expensive coats and the scent of luxe beauty products enveloping my mom in a soft cloud, but mostly I was struck by how relieved I was to see them.

I kept grabbing at my long-sleeved shirt and pulling the sleeves over my hands, an old habit from when I was feeling scared as a child. I ran up to them and blurted out "Mommy!" I wanted to bury my head in the bosom of my mom's cashmere sweater. I wanted her to take me home, buckled in the back seat of their Volvo like when I'd had a bad day at school.

"You look so frightened," she said. I nodded with a sad, closed-mouthed smile. I knew I couldn't cry because the nurses were watching, clipboard and pencils in hand, and I had to pretend like I was getting better.

I went to hug my dad. He put his arms around me loosely and gave my back a pound, like a guy hugging his buddy after a football game. "Hi, Bar." He looked at my belly, shaking his head. "You look, you look really pregnant." A twist of his mouth and bug of his eyes—it was a face I hadn't seen in years but was too familiar. I could see in that face his disgust with me, his pregnant daughter in a psych ward. What a failure I was. How unfit to be a mother.

My mom looked back and forth between us, always poised to play clean-up. In an uncharacteristic moment of strength in the face of my father's anger, I ended up asking my dad to please leave. I couldn't bear any more guilt and blame and shame. My dad just shrugged on his leather bomber jacket with a grunt, his shoulders stooped, and turned around to walk out of the ward.

I know my father's patterns, that he is cruel when he's afraid—a classic bully—but I couldn't be analytical and forgiving that morning. I am now, but not then.

For the remainder of our nightmare, though, my dad rarely showed his ugliness. And after our daughter was born, he never showed it again at all.

Throughout the next year, my father would answer hundreds of my phone calls at all times of the day, interrupting sessions with his own patients to speak with me. He would check in with doctors on my behalf. One time, later that winter, by the time dark voices had started swirling loudly around my mind, he drove to our apartment in Queens and brought me a noise machine with huge, soft head-phones to help me drown the voices out. He stayed up deep into the night digging through medical textbooks and printing out articles, desperate as we were to find a diagnosis.

———

My mom didn't want to talk about any of it, and right then, neither did I. After my dad slumped out of the ward, my mom and I looked at each other over the Zabars bag on the table. "I love you, Mommy," I said. "I love you too, sweetie," she replied. "You're my heart." We saw the baby kick beneath my shirt. She's always loved the sound of my mother's voice. The three of us. We were so sad that morning.

———

Seemingly overnight, two new disturbing symptoms surfaced. They would not leave me for more than a year. First were the lights: specifically, fluorescent overheads. Any unnatural lighting began to make my surroundings blurred and bright, giving all solid objects a sickly halo. Neon colors screamed, and blacks contrasted in lines that were hard and mean.

The second and more disturbing symptom was that everyone—from my family to people I had just met—had become body doubles of themselves, alien proxies. The strange thing was, I was aware this was happening. I knew they were still real—I didn't truly think they were aliens—but I had to live with this new demented thought distortion. I felt like it was so much worse having this separation, this knowing that what I was seeing and believing wasn't real. These new symptoms would be the start of my plummet deep into the underworld of a dissociative disorder, where I would reside for years to come.

That morning, it was as though I had slipped inside a bad dream, a bad trip, a bad movie where I couldn't escape. I closed my eyes, blinking hard, reopening them to find I was still trapped in this alternate version of reality.

I tried to grab ahold of what I knew to be true: I was Patrick's wife; I was my daughter's mother. We were real. We were a family. We had jobs, friends, a home, a life. But I was now residing in a shadow world. The ward was a horror movie set; the patients, ghosts; the doctors, mechanical clones.

I had an unfounded suspicion that the new symptoms were from the sleeping pills I had so gratefully gulped down the night before.

Something had to be causing this. It couldn't just be the way my mind worked now, could it?

A patient in the dayroom hooked his arms around his midsection and rocked back and forth, muttering. "They got me locked up man. They got me locked up."

Me too. I thought. *Me too*.

Still, I knew I had to be good. I didn't ask questions. I didn't cry. I sat politely in the dayroom with Daniel. He had found a new friend, Tyler, who was much closer to Daniel's age than I was. They played chess and watched basketball as Daniel shared his girl problems. I tried to look like I was a part of their conversation.

On the metal library cart, I found Brooke Shields's memoir, *Down Came the Rain*. I skipped to the part where she talks about having thoughts of throwing her newborn daughter against the wall, comforting myself with the thought that I wasn't there—yet.

———

It was late afternoon when Dr. Abrams came to get me for our private session.

"You look good," he said, noticing I had changed out of the paper pajamas. "Comfortable. Let's go somewhere quiet." He led me to the art room.

The room smelled comforting, oil pastels and dried paint. Outside the window, just after sunset, the sky had turned a dark blue. Dr. Abrams gestured toward a chair at the head of the table and, instead of sitting across from me, pulled a chair out for himself, just to my right.

"So," he said. "Let's start easy. How were the holidays?"

"We didn't do much celebrating," I said. "It was too hard for me to see anyone." I looked down at the table, scratched and flecked with paint. "But we did make it to dinner. We celebrated our wedding anniversary a week ago."

"Where to?" Dr. Abrams asked.

"A restaurant called Del Posto. It was where we got married." I replied.

"I know Del Posto," Dr. Abrams said crossing his arms behind his head. "Love Molto Mario."

I gave a small smile. "Dinner was good. The rest, not so much."

"Tell me about your relationship. Your marriage," he said, leaning in now and resting his elbows on the table.

"I think it's pretty clear that we love each other."

Dr. Abrams grinned. "True. He takes care of you."

"He does," I agreed.

"And before Patrick?"

"Before?"

"Other relationships?"

I shook my head. "It wasn't the same. Not like with him, like unconditional. I mean, I didn't meet Patrick until I was thirty-four. So there were, there were others. But not the same."

Dr. Abrams nodded slowly. "So this isn't your first rodeo, as they say."

I laughed a little. "I guess not."

"And sex?"

"With Patrick? In general or now?"

"Now."

"It's been a while, probably since October." I thought of our last time together, right around Halloween.

Dr. Abrams slowly nodded again. "That's a long time. Sex is important."

"I can't do anything that feels good anymore. I can't even read a book."

"Big reader?"

"It's my only hobby," I said.

"Why do you think you won't you let yourself do anything that feels good?"

"Punishing myself, I guess?"

"Punishing yourself, why?"

"For messing up already. I dyed my hair." I reached for my braid. "I checked myself in here. I'm already ruining her life, and I haven't even started."

"I think . . . ," Dr. Abrams began, "I think you're hard on yourself. I think you dyed your hair because you were feeling awful and you wanted to feel good. I think you checked yourself in here because you wanted to sleep and you knew that's what you and the baby needed. I'd argue that you're a good mom."

I smiled, grateful now. "You think so?"

"I do. And I think you need to start getting ready for the baby. This weekend, I have an assignment. I want you to sketch the baby's room. Make a list of the things you need. Think about what color you want to paint the nursery."

For a moment, my mind bloomed. I would paint the nursery listening to Motown and wearing overalls. I would sit on the floor between Patrick's legs as he learned to massage my lower back during prenatal class. I would open gifts of onesies and board books and embroidered blankets at a baby shower with a big sheet cake and bows from the presents in my hair. Dr. Abrams made me feel hopeful.

"And we're going to adjust the dosage of your Zoloft," Dr. Abrams said. "One hundred and fifty milligrams."

"That sounds high," I said. "My other psychiatrist just raised it, and it made me feel worse."

"It will make you feel better. Three weeks, you'll be back to yourself. You'll see."

I couldn't help but trust him.

Chapter Nine

Over the weekend, the ward went quiet. It was snowing outside for the first time that winter, and it really started to pile up. My heart broke. The baby and I had to share our first snowstorm together in a psych ward. I spread my fingers over my belly and watched the flakes fall through the safety-glass windows.

The staff who had been there all week, including the team, were home for the weekend and were replaced with a crew who affected the attitude of bored substitute teachers, playing Candy Crush on their phones or tossing around ideas for upcoming vacations, cruises, package deals. They wanted nothing to do with us, and that was fine— they were lazy about taking notes and making ticks. Even though no one was really paying attention, I still went to yoga and arts and crafts and drum circle. I borrowed a magic marker from the nurses' station to sketch out the nursery like Dr. Abrams had suggested. I didn't cry. I didn't ask questions. I was quiet and good.

When Patrick came that night, I pressed my forehead against his while we spoke. The closer I could get to him, the less alien he became. I could sacrifice anyone else, but Patrick had to remain himself. I couldn't lose him to my delusions. I kept asking him if he thought Dr. Abrams had lied, if they were going to keep holding me hostage, if they weren't ever going to let me go home.

We were caught back inside my repetitive loops, my catastrophic prophesies. Underneath the heaviness of our dread.

During dinner, we faced one another, squeezing each other's hands tightly. A woman with bleached hair and an open-backed gown sat facing the wall, a plastic tray of meat loaf and gravy congealing before her. She screamed until she was gasping for breath, but no one ever came to help.

———

On Monday morning, the team was back, but Dr. Abrams wouldn't catch my eye. I sat on the couch shaking and silent as I flipped through the pages of my Brooke Shields memoir with sweaty fingers. The team held the power to keep me there longer, and that fact gripped me with terror. I wanted to go home.

———

Dr. Abrams didn't approach me with any news about my release until almost noon, when Patrick was already at the hospital for visiting hours.

We were brought into a small, cold office and joined by a social worker. As we faced one another in folding chairs, it was the social worker who mostly spoke, outlining the terms of my release. Dr.

Abrams sat back, silently observing, clinical now, the warmth gone. The social worker detailed the final condition of my release. I was to see a reproductive psychiatrist whose services were $750 out of pocket and obtain a signed form verifying my visit.

Dr. Abrams finally spoke. "How do you feel?" he asked.

"I feel better," I said, both lying and wishing fiercely that it was true.

Dr. Abrams looked over at Patrick. "How do you think she is? Would you say she's back to herself?"

"I think so," Patrick replied, nodding. "I hope so."

Dr. Abrams regarded both of us for a moment and then spoke. "I think if it were up to me, I would have kept her here longer. Just to make sure that we were out of the woods. To make sure she was really getting some rest. But even so, I wish you both the best of luck. Please make sure to see the reproductive psychiatrist before the end of the week." He stood up and shook both of our hands.

I didn't say goodbye to anyone, not even Daniel. I walked out of the room and down the corridor with my head down, not looking back at the place that would live on in my nightmares, both awake and asleep, for years to come.

———

Years later, when I received the notes from my stay at the ward, I discovered that Dr. Abrams thought I had been manipulating him with my "superficial brightness." He described me as being "inappropriately flirtatious" with him, seeking attention with my "seductive body language" and "different tone of voice" when communicating with him. My oversexualized, attention-seeking ways were also noted in my interactions with Patrick. That we had kissed when saying goodbye in front of the nurses' station. That we sat too close to each other. That we leaned against each other when we walked down the hall. I read the notes, remembering his comments on my body in my tight maternity clothes, the questions he asked about sex with my husband, leaning in closer to me as I spoke.

Patrick and I were both devastated when we read these words. Dr. Abrams, in our minds, had been one of the good ones, one of the smart ones. We had kept his words in our minds and carried them with us for a long time. We had remembered his voice. We had remembered his name.

After reading those notes, I took to my bed and lay down for a long time, feeling coated in an invisible layer of filth on the outside, my chest pounding with rage from within. I may have been a lot of things during my stay on the ward: frightened, estranged from my loved ones, dissociated, sick. Pregnant. Suicidal. But I was definitely, absolutely incapable of being seductive. My memories may be muddled or have gaps, but this is something I know with a certainty as clear as glass.

———

If I were to retrace my steps through the ward now, to wind the figure eights, to pace the halls, to trace the loops repeatedly, would I still find it to be the house of horrors that remains in my mind? Or would it just be a place where I ate and slept and spent countless hours sitting on a cracked leather couch, waiting for a doctor to see me?

All I knew was it was another stop on my freefall. My cries for help landing me in places where I would rest in a brief moment of hope before another trapdoor opened and I continued my descent, further and further down.

For months after my discharge, I woke up each day terrified. I had a ritual: Before getting out of bed, I had to lay my entire body down on top of Patrick's, press my face to his and make him repeat the assurance that we had made the right decision the morning we took the subway to the psych ER; that it hadn't made me worse; that I'd never be going back. I had to complete this ritual several times in a row, until I could convince myself he was telling me the truth. I asked Patrick what he had thought would happen once I got out of the hospital. "I thought you would be better," he said. "I thought we could be back to normal once I brought you home."

———

Patrick stayed in touch with my principal, Richard, throughout the hospitalization. Richard has known me for over a decade and cares about me as a teacher and as a person—my co-workers joke about me about being his favorite. The boss's pet. He was frightened for us and told us several times that he couldn't fathom what we were going through. He had all the holiday gifts I received from my students— the Ferrero Rochers, the gift cards—delivered in a box to our house.

I had barely entered my classroom since Thanksgiving and had long since run out of sick days. There were no more numbers Richard could fudge or dates he could move around. If I missed any more days of teaching, my salary would be docked. At 3:30 p.m. on January 9, Patrick and I signed out. At 7:30 a.m. on January 10, I would be returning to work.

Chapter Ten

Seven hundred and fifty dollars out of pocket is on the cheaper end for a consultation with a "repro psych," and waiting lists can be months long. When we had asked our ob-gyn for a referral for a reproductive psychiatrist early on in the pregnancy, he gave us the number for a physician who prescribed nutritional supplements and a grain-free diet plan with no nightshade vegetables—and no medication. She cost $1,500 per session.

Reproductive psychiatrists are wealthy, well-educated white women. If you are lucky enough to pay the entrance fee into their exclusive club, you are probably a wealthy, well-educated white woman too.

As mandated, I went to see the reproductive psychiatrist assigned to me by the social worker a few days after I had returned from the hospital. I took the subway to her hushed penthouse office suite on the Upper East Side. It was a January day where the city was all gray and stone, the tall buildings leaning in on me. I'd lived in New York City for nearly twenty years—it belonged to me. But that afternoon, I felt small and lost in the city's cold maze.

The doctor had the brusque demeanor unique to chic New York women who are used to getting what they want. Even so, she was sympathetic, and I could sense that beneath her all-business exterior, she was a little afraid for me. I repeated my story, now with the addition of my brief institutionalization.

My daughter's due date was on April 6, 2017—the day after my birthday. I had thirteen weeks to find a way to reverse the course of my insanity and get ready to be a mother. The doctor understood our urgency. She also understood that I would not be able to afford her.

That afternoon, she spent most of our forty-five-minute meeting on the phone with other psychiatrists in her network, fast-talking in a broad, Long Island accent, like she was a day trader and I was a stock to sell. No luck. No one would take me for under $500 per session. As our time together came to a close, she did promise to keep trying to find me help. She would put my case on a message board where psychiatrists throughout the city could read about the undiagnosable pregnant woman who was too poor to afford their treatment and bid on me online instead.

Before I left her office, I told her I still wasn't sleeping. It had now been almost a month and a half, and the most I had slept was three hours per night—and that had happened only once. "Okay." She leaned in closer. "I'm going to prescribe you something that is gonna Knock. *You. Out,*" she said in the manner of someone offering up a line in the bathroom of a Downtown loft party. "You'll be sleeping like a baby in no time."

I left the appointment with no psychiatrist to treat me, still no real diagnosis, but I did have a new prescription for 50 milligrams of Seroquel. An antipsychotic. And knock me out it did. The next morning, Patrick had to lightly slap my face several times so I could wake up, get out of bed, and go to work.

———

Each morning, I opened my eyes and checked to see if the world had gone back to normal. It never did. Then I'd lie on top of Patrick and repeat the same questions (*Had we made the right choice? Would the baby be okay? Was I going to have to live like this forever?*) until we had to get ready for work.

Once I finally got out of bed, I'd quickly pull on stretched-out maternity leggings and Patrick's baggy sweaters. I avoided looking at my body as much as possible. Sometimes, I could get it together enough to take a shower. I used to love clothes and makeup and took care in dressing for my day, but now I wanted no one to notice me; I was so ashamed of what I had become.

I either spent $15 on a seven-minute car ride to work or I walked, my head down, the icy January cold freezing the tips of my hair.

When I entered the school building, I was immediately thrown deeper into my alternate reality, the brightly colored hallways and cheap fluorescent bulbs making me feel as though my eyes were rolling in the back of my skull.

My teaching assistant that year, Karina, was sweet and young, with an open, round face and glossy black hair that reached the small of her back. Karina was in the last semester of her master's program, and after spending the day at school with me, she had to head to the city for classes that ran late into the evening.

Usually, I could manage to read my class a story or help a student with a writing assignment, but mostly, Karina took over and did everything. She got paid half of what I was making, but she stayed quiet and never complained to anyone. I wish I could have done more to thank her. My students' faces—with their big, long-lashed eyes and soft, peach fuzzy cheeks—turned ghoulish in the fluorescent light of the classroom, and it was too hard for me to look.

Just like in the hospital, I couldn't sit still. A co-worker of mine remembers seeing me wandering the halls of the school every afternoon while I was supposed to be teaching. I left class each hour and made frantic carousels of phone calls while hiding under the stairwell or in the janitor's closet: Patrick, my mom, my dad, sometimes Celine, sometimes Patrick's sister, Leigh. I gripped the phone tight, my ear sweating against the receiver, my eyes closed. Finally, one of them would say something that calmed me down and I could make it through the rest of the hour.

I don't believe in God, but I prayed like an earnest schoolgirl for what Dr. Abrams had told me in our therapy session to be true: that in three weeks' time, the medicine would kick in and I would be feeling back to normal. At the three-week mark, though, I was worse than ever. If the Zoloft wasn't working, then I probably wasn't depressed. If the Seroquel only seemed to help me sleep, then I probably wasn't psychotic. What was wrong with me?

My suicidal ideations were growing more and more elaborate by the day, fantasies of rivers and backpacks filled with heavy books. I had stopped being able to ride subways and would ask taxi drivers to take the tunnels. If we had to go over a bridge, I squeezed my eyes shut.

I wasn't hearing voices, exactly, but certain words or phrases or snippets of songs got stuck in my head and repeated through my mind in the dark tone of an announcer presenting a horror movie. Mainly, the words were names of psychiatric drugs, all new to me—*trazodone*, *risperidone*—or lyrics from songs that contained the word "suicide." *Beautiful girl . . . you'll have me suicidal, suicidal.* Another word that floated through from time to time was *claro*, or "clear," an expression of the deepest wish for how I wanted to feel. As I lay in bed at night, especially if there was a fan on, I could clearly hear the faint crackling of newscasters on an old-timey radio. I'd put the pillow over my head and wait until the Seroquel kicked in so I could escape into sleep. Any last vestiges of hope were disappearing. I could hold on until after the baby was born, but after that, all I wanted was to no longer exist.

———

Mostly, my friends and co-workers left me alone, scared for me and scared of me. Two of my close work friends were pregnant, and one had recently had a baby. I couldn't be anywhere near them; they were such a strong reminder of my failure. I loved my friends at work—most of us were founding teachers at the school and had been together in the trenches of New York City public education for several years.

Each lunchtime, we brought our foulest language, our dirtiest stories, tidbits of gossip rolling around in our mouths like sucking candy. I regressed to a wild teen with them in the best way, laughing until we doubled over in the kiddie-sized plastic chairs. We delighted in our friendship, in our short windows of time together.

Now I preferred to eat lunch alone in the classroom, staring out the window as the car-carrier trucks drove by on their way to deliveries on Northern Boulevard, the shiny cars casting red and yellow shadows on the classroom walls.

During the lunch hours alone at my desk, I did a lot of googling. I searched for pregnant women who have been treated in psychiatric hospitals (a few), pregnant women who have experienced suicidal ideation (more than a few), and reviews of psych wards (many—there are a number of sites heralding themselves as "A Yelp for Psychiatric Facilities," as well as several actual Yelp reviews of psychiatric facilities). Most reviews begin with the patient's often grotesque mistreatment by ward staff and end with how much more traumatized and unwell they felt when they were released.

My greatest fear was that I was hurting the baby, through my stress, through the medications I was taking. When you are pregnant, the internet is not your friend, even if you are in the soundest state of mind. My ob-gyn constantly implored me to stop self-diagnosing, saying that if I wanted to find research articles that stated, "Apples cause autism in unborn children," they existed. I couldn't stop though: Each day, I went deeper down the hole, reopening the wound.

I kept circling back to the *New York Times* and the *New Yorker*, which had each published a few pieces linking autism or severe ADHD in children to their exposure to psychiatric drugs in utero. If our daughter was going to be on the autism spectrum or have any learning differences or attention deficit disorder, it was fine; we would love her for who she was, no matter what. I had taught for ten years at this point and knew that loving kids on all points of the spectrum was very, very easy. But it was a lot of work too. For the parents, for their teachers, and for the child. And if she had to suffer in any way, I had to live with the fact that it was my fault. I was the one who got sick. I was the one who took the medications. I was the one who couldn't properly care for my baby, and she hadn't even been born yet. And I couldn't live with that. There was no way I could bear it.

I also researched my symptoms. The crushing depression, but also the acute pain of bright lights, the alien proxies, the unfamiliarity of the world and the unrecognizability of myself. The loops. The fact that I was hyperaware of these symptoms happening, that they weren't occurring in a fugue state. That I had a front-row seat to my psychological demise.

My searches kept landing on a disorder I had never heard of before: depersonalization-derealization disorder. And I kept finding my truth. *The feeling that you're observing yourself from outside your body or you have a sense that things around you aren't real, or both . . . you may feel like you're living in a dream . . . alienated from or unfamiliar with your surroundings . . . feeling emotionally disconnected from people you care about, as if you were separated by a glass wall . . . surroundings appear distorted, blurry, colorless, two-dimensional or artificial . . . distortions in perception of time . . . distortions of distance and the size and shape of objects.*

Scrolling down the pages for the treatment plan, my heart pounded with longing, but I was always met with the same death knell: *There are no medications specifically approved to treat depersonalization-derealization disorder. Contact your primary care provider.*

Unable to help myself, though, I dug deeper. Peeking through my fingers like a child watching a horror movie, I sifted through articles, Facebook groups, threads on Reddit, books on Amazon.

The books had titles like *Stranger to Myself* or *Feeling Unreal*. On their covers were pictures of crying clowns, black tears dripping down painted white faces. The Facebook group greeted visitors with a blown-up picture of Edvard Munch's *The Scream* as it's cover photo. Images posted at the tops of articles showed young men and women trapped inside hallucinatory fractal designs, like darker versions of a poster you might find on a college dorm room wall.

I learned that DPDR was a dissociative disorder. The only dissociative disorder I had ever heard of was dissociative identity disorder, more commonly known as multiple personality disorder. I knew that once you had a dissociative disorder, there was no coming back.

I compared the sites on dissociative disorders with the pages and pages of peripartum and postpartum mood disorders. The pictures I saw there were of pretty, long-haired women wearing yoga clothes and dejected faces as they cradled plump babies. There were lists of medications, support groups, doctors, promises that things would get better. *Please*, I thought, *please let that be me.*

But the world of dissociative disorders continued to reach out its long, sharp-nailed and crooked finger, beckoning me to come and join them where I really belonged.

Please, God, no, I silently begged. And I slammed my computer shut.

———

After being home from the hospital for almost a month, we received some news. A doctor from the message board had seen my case and was willing to take me on. She was much less expensive than the other reproductive psychiatrists (it wasn't her main specialty), but she would see us for $325 per session, twice a week, out of pocket. For most psychiatrists in New York City, this is the going rate. Four years later, we are still paying off the years of our descent into hell, most of which we had to purchase on a credit card.

The psychiatrist's name was Dr. Cook, and we liked her immediately. She had long, frizzy hair and glasses that often slipped off the slope of her nose. She wore tank tops even in the winter, showing off her arms, ropy from her daily swims.

Dr. Cook had a blunt and casual way of speaking and didn't mind sharing some personal information (she had a daughter she referred to as "G," she swam daily, she lived in a small apartment on the Upper West Side).

Each session was a collaboration, a plan to get me better. There were none of the staring contests typical of most therapy sessions— mini seances where the psychiatrist tries to summon the patient to speak. And she had Patrick sit in the office next to me every time we met, something both he and I deeply appreciated.

During the sessions, they busted my chops. Their camaraderie made me feel a little wounded, but mostly it brought some normalcy into the forty-five minutes we spent together. When I tried my questioning loops with Dr. Cook, she wrinkled her nose and pushed up her glasses. Then she turned to Patrick and asked, "Is she always like this?" She put me in my place, and I deserved it. Yes, I was sick—but, truthfully, my maudlin repetitions were getting kind of annoying.

A few visits in, I confessed my dark secret: that I believed I had depersonalization-derealization disorder. The rare mental illness no medication could cure. Throughout our work with Dr. Cook, we had run through a few diagnoses: bipolar disorder, peripartum psychosis, major depressive disorder. None of them were the perfect fit—and none had responded to medication.

On the day of my confession, Dr. Cook opened her copy of the DSM-V. We went through each disorder, reading the symptoms. No match. Then we got to depersonalization-derealization disorder, and she read the description of me.

———

Dr. Cook kept trying, but depersonalization-derealization disorder was far from her field of expertise. Or any psychiatrist's field of expertise, for that matter. There are only a few doctors in the entire country who specialize in DPDR and, at the time, only one in New York.

The doctor I found was based in the city, her office just a cab ride across town from Dr. Cook's. She specialized in DPDR and had even written one of the seminal books on the disorder. I bought her book, but I never read it. Whatever she had to say, I was too afraid to find out.

Even though it was far afield for her, Dr. Cook wouldn't give up on us. She worked with us and she worked hard, yet she was reluctant to diagnose me solely with depersonalization-derealization disorder, wanting instead to treat it as a symptom of my depression. DPDR more commonly shows up as a symptom of other disorders—like the lucid dream state that ebbed and flowed during the panic attacks of my twenties.

Eventually, I let it go and stopped bringing up DPDR. I was willing away the diagnosis that I knew to be true, wanting desperately to have a disorder that could be medicated or even cured. If Dr. Cook thought it was a symptom of depression, then I would believe her. I was about to be a mother. I needed to believe I could get well.

Dr. Cook attacked our case from all angles. She arranged for me to be analyzed by Genomind, a company that processes your genetic makeup and uses the information to find the best drugs to prescribe for your specific disorder (useless and expensive). She made us an appointment with a psychiatrist who practiced hypnosis (useless and very, very expensive). She was on the phone with my ob-gyn every single day as they discussed different medication options that were safe for the baby. She had my ob-gyn see me for sonograms twice a week so I could be reassured that despite the drugs, the baby was growing and thriving. That she was doing okay.

———

The weeks passed. I went on and off different medications. I squeezed my eyes shut in taxis as they hurtled over the Queensboro Bridge on my way to doctor's appointments in Manhattan every day after work. I wanted to get well, but my mind wandered, plotting ways I could escape after the baby was born. The bleach under the kitchen sink. The bottle of antifreeze in our entryway. Ten minutes of holding my head underwater in the bathtub.

———

We still signed up for the birthing class at the hospital. We still had a baby shower. My parents took us to shop for furniture for the nursery. Patrick bought pale lavender paint at Home Depot and decorated the baby's room, alone.

I was one of those women who pretended she was too cool to care, but truthfully, I had fantasized about weddings and showers and babymoons since I can remember. I daydreamed about mobiles and ballerina music boxes and nightlights that projected constellations onto the nursery ceiling. I made lists of names.

I mourned the loss of these fantasies, then and for a long time after.

We only made it to the first three birthing classes because I couldn't bear to be inside a hospital, the lights and smells and uniformed attendants bringing me to humiliating tears in front of the other parents in the group.

For our babymoon, all I could manage was riding the E train out to Rockaway Beach on a Monday afternoon. It was the last week of February, and we spent our few hours together walking down the boardwalk while I silently cried, trying hard not to spoil the day.

The shower was held at my good friend Amy's home in Ridgewood. We only invited our parents, close friends, my youngest brother, Alex, and my sister-in-law, Leigh. I wasn't involved in any of the planning; Amy and my mom took care of everything since I was incapable of handling much of anything by that point. All our friends came, some with small children of their own. Our friends were tender and gentle and brought sweet gifts, but I couldn't stay for the whole party. I went home after about an hour. It was too difficult for me to be around big groups of people, especially parents of young children.

At the shower, my friend Sara told me about how when she was pregnant with her son, right before he was born, she would spend hours sorting through his tiny clothes—little corduroy overalls or onesies printed with baby owls or turtles. She would hold his blankets to her face, rubbing their silky edges, and refold them carefully, placing them back in the drawer.

I thought of this story every single day. Our baby's clothes and gifts were in a pile on the bedroom floor. I couldn't bear to touch them. I didn't deserve to.

I grew bigger and bigger as I tried to shrink further inside myself.

At about two weeks before my due date, Dr. Cook had some news. She and my ob-gyn had discussed the option of inducing labor. Once the baby was born, we would be able to try different medications that would not have been safe to take during the pregnancy.

With the plan of induction, a mystical notion was conjured and began floating between the doctors and our families. The collective idea was that I might just return to normal once the baby was born. That maybe the pregnancy itself had been the problem all along.

And so, it was decided. On Wednesday, March 30, at 1:00 a.m., we had an appointment to give birth to our baby girl.

Chapter Eleven

Up until the night before she was born, our daughter had a different name.

In the summer of 2011, I had returned from a three-year stint teaching in Marrakech, Morocco. I was smitten with the country, the culture, and the people. My time there defined me as the kind of woman I had always dreamed of becoming: adventurous, brave, worldly, carefree.

Back home in Brooklyn, my journey had given me a new confidence—especially with romantic interests—that I had been lacking before. Now, I had a story to tell. When I met Patrick in the summer of 2012, I recounted my adventures for him while we sat on the fire escape, a pack of Camel Lights and a few tall boys between us, the dense city heat relenting as the sun set and we talked into the night. My stories about Morocco were one of the things that drew Patrick to me and kept him there, listening.

When it came time to name our baby, I wanted her to have a Moroccan name, to bless her with the mystical combination of strength and magic I associated with my time there. By the time I was pregnant, and we had been together for four years, Patrick had grown a little tired of my Morocco tales, but he appreciated the motive behind my name choices. Plus, he liked the names I had picked: Noor and Camille.

The meaning of Noor in Arabic is "the light," and this moved me. The name conjured an image of the glowing blaze of the sun at dawn. As much as the name moved me, though, neither Patrick nor I had any shred of Moroccan DNA floating around in us and knew it was a little pretentious for a couple of thirty-something white Brooklynites to co-opt a Moroccan name for their daughter. And so we choose the more-common name, Camille, as her first name. Noor would be her lovely secret, hidden in the middle.

We imagined that as a woman, she would be Camille. Long legged and elegant with dark hair pulled back in a bun as she swept into galleries and law firms and engineering labs for job interviews. But as our little girl, she would be Cammy, mismatched socks and scraped knees, pigtails swinging when she ran through the sprinklers at the playground.

We talked about Cammy all the time. Cammy likes when Mommy eats mint chocolate chip ice cream. Cammy's going to love playing catch with her dad. Cammy will look so sweet in her red stroller. We bought stuffed camels for her crib, the perfect mascot.

On the evening before the induction, Patrick came in from work and didn't even take off his coat before pronouncing, "I hate 'Cammy.'"

"Why?" I asked, staring up at him from my seat at the dining room table.

Cammy was sickeningly sweet, he said. It was cheap, it was tawdry. And Camille was pretentious. An unwanted cloud of perfume sprayed on you at the department store. He didn't ever want to meet a Camille. He didn't ever want to see the name in print. The name Camille was a curse, a bad luck charm that would not be our daughter's burden to bear.

"What about Noor-ah?" he asked. "Nora."

"Yes," I replied, smiling. "Nora. That's our little girl."

Her name originates from the Latin *honora*, meaning "honor." Nora, as a derivative in its Irish and Hebrew origins, though, means "light." She would be our tiny beacon, our new day.

———

I had never once given thought to the idea of actually giving birth: if it would be painful, if I would cry, if there would be complications. By that point, I didn't care about anything. I had hardly asked my ob-gyn any questions about the birthing process, but I asked Dr. Cook hundreds of times if she really believed that it was true—that once Nora was born, I would return to myself.

I had no birthing plan. They could drug me, cut me open, put me in a bathtub; I just needed her out of my body so I could get on some stronger meds and start getting better. I couldn't even think about my baby by then. Mental illness made me selfish.

———

The day of the induction became a countdown. We would call a car service at 11:00 p.m. to bring us to the hospital for our 1:00 a.m. appointment. The rest of the day was ours to fill, our last hours of being alone, together.

Those long hours before our appointment were surprisingly sweet and languid. We were both quiet and mellow. It was warm outside, the beginning of spring. The clocks had just moved forward an hour, and the new light cast the neighborhood in a softer glow.

We took a walk to the bookstore and went to the supermarket to pick out healthy snacks to eat while we waited for me to go into labor, filling a cart with graham crackers, strawberries, and fresh-squeezed orange juice. Back at home, Patrick lay behind me on the couch with his arm draped over my belly and we tried to nap, the late afternoon sun seeping through the lace curtains, making patterns on the living room walls.

I still watched the day unfold while separated from the world inside my glass box, but I was calm. It would all be over soon.

At 11:00 p.m. we brought the baby's car seat and a bag packed with tiny pajamas down to our front stoop to call the car. On the stoop, our downstairs neighbor smoked a cigarette. The three of us stood silently until the headlights of the town car pulled into view.

The waiting room of the Labor and Delivery unit is soothing, unlike its counterpart in the psych ER, four floors below. New Age music tinkles in over invisible speakers, and bottled water and snacks are displayed in a small glass fridge. Cushioned seats are arranged in pairs, separated by tables adorned with artificial succulents. Abstract art in pastel tones hangs on the walls.

Women enter with their partners, holding their bellies and grinning in disbelief. "I think my water broke! We just took a cab here!" they exclaim to the receptionists. The receptionists beam back, joining in their happy bubble. The partners have their arms around the mothers' shoulders. Everyone seems so proud.

Patrick and I made an odd sight in the Labor and Delivery waiting room that night. I sat next to him on the cushioned chairs, my face pressed into his canvas jacket, unable to look. I was still terrified of hospitals.

When the receptionist called our name, we walked over to her desk and told her we were scheduled for an induction. When she asked why I was being induced, I leaned forward and murmured that I had severe depression and needed to be on stronger medication as soon as possible. I couldn't bear the humiliation of any of the joyful couples in the room overhearing me. The receptionist raised her eyebrows and made a note on a chart, her mouth in a hard, taut line.

———

There are many reasons to induce labor, but severe peripartum mental illness is not usually one of them. I had to shame myself by recounting my story, this time to even more strangers than in the psych ER: residents on their rounds, nurses clocking into their shifts. As I spoke, the raised eyebrows and pursed lips on the doctors' and nurses' faces spoke silent recriminations. This is not the way a new life is supposed to begin

In a chastising tone, a nurse broke down the induction process to me. She moved around the room, fiddling with different wires and setting up instruments on trays as she ran rapid-fire down the list of steps we would take to bring my daughter into the world. As she spoke, she didn't look at me once.

"Okay, step one; we're gonna insert dinoprostone. This'll dilate your cervix. If that doesn't work, we move onto step two: a balloon catheter. It's a device with a small inflatable balloon on the end. We blow up the balloon to dilate your cervix. That doesn't work, we start the Pitocin drip. That's gonna induce the contractions. Contractions don't start, we raise the dosage. Then we break the sac by inserting a small hook to rupture it. If you don't respond to any of these interventions, we do a C-section. Any questions?"

I knew about Pitocin, but hooks and balloons? At that point, I realized I should have done more research and felt the now-familiar gut punch of guilt. Look at how selfish I was, choosing to give birth to my baby this way. Another decision to second guess, to add to my ruminations. Was I trying to take the easy way out? Or was I desperate to get better for my daughter?

I'm not a fainter, but after the nurse described the induction procedure, I came close. My breathing became shallow and sweat beaded on my upper lip and at my temples, sending tiny rivulets down my cheeks.

Finally, the nurse stopped setting up and looked at me—my ashen, sweaty face. Then she glanced over at Patrick. "She take her meds this morning?" asking him as though I wasn't in the room. "Yeah," he responded. "She gets anxious sometimes." "Hm," the nurse said, like we ought to know better. "I'm gonna get the anesthesiologist for the epidural. Get this show on the road." She walked out the door, and we never saw her again.

———

The window in the hospital room faced north, and I watched dawn break over the same slice of sky I had stared at from my cot in the psych ER back in January. The labor and delivery nurse came in and closed the blinds, imploring me to sleep.

I had been awake for almost twenty-four hours and had only been allowed to sip broth and juice. The hunger and exhaustion, combined with the dim glow coming in through the closed curtains, made me feel as though I was existing within a fever dream. The bottom half of my body was completely numb from the epidural, and I observed with a detached interest as my catheter bag filled with my pee.

The day inched forward as I cycled through the steps of the induction; the dinoprostone, the balloon catheter. The nurse who was with us for most of the day was an older woman with glasses and a soothing Russian accent. She came in every half hour or so to change my catheter bag and chatted with us for a few minutes as I sipped Dixie cups of apple juice.

In the late afternoon, before the shift change, she came in for the last time to say goodbye. She leaned in close to me and brushed my sweaty bangs off my forehead. "I read your chart, Mommy. You are strong, too strong to be depressed," she said softly rolling her "R"s. She reached for my hand, stuck with a needle that was hooked up to an IV. "You do not need to take medication. You need to stay natural, for the baby. Something I do to help with depression is Kundalini yoga. Please try that, instead of medication, Mommy. For the baby." She looked up at Patrick. "Good luck to you, Daddy," she said and then back down at me, "and good luck to you, Mommy." She gave my hand a gentle squeeze before turning around to leave.

———

By 5:00 that afternoon, I was only dilated 1 centimeter. My ob-gyn had arrived at the hospital and prepared me for the Pitocin drip, which would hopefully bring on the contractions that would dilate me further. This would be a process that could potentially take hours and, even with the epidural numbing the lower half of my body, would be extremely painful.

Nearly every woman I know who has had a child, including my own mother, has given birth via cesarian section. Since these were the stories of birth that had been passed down to me, in my mind I was sure I would be having a C-section too. I figured we could probably skip the whole Pitocin part and just wheel me over to the OR to get it over with.

After the drip started, I began contracting almost immediately. The baby's head was wedged all the way to the lower right-hand side of my pelvis, and I still wince at the exquisite pain this caused, her head rubbing my insides raw every time a contraction wave flowed through me.

The pain was more intense than I had imagined, and I heard animal moans fill the room, realizing they were coming from me. Pitocin is supposed to produce painful contractions, but this was beyond any of our expectations. And I was beginning to regain feeling in my legs. The epidural that had been injected into my lower back at 1:00 a.m. the night before had been given too early, and its effects were quickly fading. Already on the Pitocin drip, it was too late to inject another dose. The birth would happen without any buffer between the pain and me.

Each time my doctor came in to check on me, I had dilated another centimeter. By a little after seven that evening, I had gone from one centimeter to ten centimeters in under two hours. Once we hit ten centimeters, my doctor came over to stand beside my bed. Instead of his usual collared shirt and tie beneath a white lab coat, he was dressed in jeans and a gray T-shirt with a gold guitar printed on the front. "All right," he said, looking straight into my eyes. "You're going to get ready to push. Don't worry about what anyone has told you before about pushing. This is between you and me. Patrick is going to hold one leg, and the nurse is going to hold the other, and each time you feel a contraction coming, you're going to push down against it. You ready?" Aside from the shock I felt at learning I would not be delivering our daughter via C-section, I felt appreciative of the heightened drama produced by my doctor's outfit and high school football coach speech. Mostly, though, I felt the pain, finally strong enough to match physically what I had felt emotionally for all these months, and it made me feel like a warrior. I was ready to push.

Patrick and I rarely speak of the horrors that befell us during that year, but the story of Nora's birth is one we tell with pride and awe.

The nurse who helped me give birth to Nora and who stayed with us in the hours after was ethereally beautiful. Young and willowy, she wore her long hair loose, down to her waist, and had delicate tattoos on her forearms. I was delirious with pain and adrenaline and exhaustion, but I swore I could feel the empathy and light radiating from her soul. Her name was Claire.

Patrick hooked his arms around my right leg and Claire gripped onto my left. They would look over me and nod at one another each time the monitor beeped its alert that a contraction was coming. They were the perfect coaches, calm and steady, yelling out words of encouragement with every push. As Patrick would describe to friends and family later, I was a real "champ" throughout the labor and delivery. I had started pushing at 7:36. By 8:06, Nora came into the world. I felt like I had finally done something right.

A sense of spiritual mysticism enshrouds the moment Nora was born, for Patrick and me both. I had the sensation that we were floating within a starlit planetarium, inside the hazy nebula of the Big Bang. Patrick, who had watched Nora's head emerge, was consumed by the notion that appears in almost all religions, legends, and myths: that he had witnessed God create life out of clay.

Nora stopped crying the instant she was placed in my arms, and right away she opened her eyes. She had long, tapered fingers, and with them, she reached for my face. All I could think was, *It was only you, this whole time!* Many mothers who suffer from peripartum and postpartum mental illnesses experience the agonizing symptom of being unable to connect with their baby. I am fortunate that this was not the case for me. From the moment she reached for my face, we both knew: I was her mommy and she was my girl.

———

Although our doctor recommended that we let Nora sleep in the nursery that first night so I could rest, I wouldn't let her out of my arms. She was a little shrimp at just over seven pounds, but she felt solid and strong. Patrick and I alternated between feeding her tiny bottles of formula—I was not allowed to breastfeed due to the benzodiazepines I was taking. Throughout the night, I kept checking: Did it work? Was I cured? I couldn't tell with the adrenaline and oxytocin flowing through me, but I had a spark of hope. Maybe I had experienced the miracle we were all hoping for.

By the time morning came and the harsh light filled the hospital room, I knew the miracle hadn't occurred. The sounds of the hospital coming to life—the chatting nurses, the beeps of the monitors, the ringing phones—were like an assault. Doctors, nurses, physician's assistants, even maternity photographers came into our room, knocking sharply and entering without waiting for our reply. They had forms to fill out, tests to perform, blood to draw. I wanted to cover my eyes to shield myself against their presence, like they were characters from a horror movie.

When my ob-gyn came in later in the morning to congratulate us, he was back in his lab coat and tie. "You did great," he said, gently taking Nora from my arms to hold her, bouncing a little as he looked down at her wrinkled face. "She's beautiful."

"She is," I said, smiling wanly. I saw him differently that morning; no longer the T-shirt–wearing coach of the night before, he had returned to his alien proxy, unfamiliar to me, a sickly halo surrounding him.

"It was a rough pregnancy. But you made it," he said, handing Nora back to me. "Things are going to get better now. You're going to be a great mom." If only that were true.

———

We brought Nora home from the hospital two days later, on April 1, a raw and rainy day. She was zipped up in a fuzzy white suit and wore a red knit cap with bear ears sewn on, too big for her tiny head. In the car, rain slid down the windows in sheets. I sobbed in silence, not taking my eyes off Nora's sleeping face in her car seat as we crossed the Queensboro Bridge.

Chapter Twelve

During that first week home, I didn't take any pictures, I didn't make any announcements on Facebook, I didn't answer the phone for our friends and family who called throughout the days and nights to wish us congratulations. I stayed in bed, my mother and Patrick taking turns comforting me as I keened, repeating to them how much I wanted to die. In any picture of me from Nora's first week home, I look like I'm already gone—my eyes bugged out and blank, my lips pulled back in a corpse's smile.

My breasts throbbed, spurting out streams of milk I couldn't use, another reminder of all my failures. Patrick took over all the feedings, getting up every two hours throughout the night to give Nora her little bottles of formula. I snuck extra Ativan, ensuring that I couldn't wake out of my drugged sleep, where I wanted to remain. I finally had my dream life: a gentle husband, a beautiful daughter, and look what I had done; I had ruined everything. Nora deserved a better mommy; Patrick deserved a better wife. The least I could do was leave so they could go and find her.

———

The day after Nora was born, Dr. Cook called to find out how we were doing, but I don't remember speaking with her. I was angry with her, with Patrick, with my ob-gyn—with anyone who had made me believe that after Nora's birth, I would be better. How wrong they had been, how cruel to have dangled that jewel of hope in front of me. No one had even adjusted my medication. The ideas to make me well that had held so much promise before Nora's birth seemed to have been abandoned. I was on my own, unmoored on my queen-size bed.

I was furious, and bereft, yes, but I was also maudlin and dramatic. In the evenings during Nora's first week home, Patrick and I tried to watch the last season of *Girls*, normally a pleasure for me and a guilty pleasure for Patrick—he couldn't help himself from cracking up during each episode.

In the last season, Lena Dunham's character had become pregnant, and in the finale she gave birth to her adorable baby, followed by a happy commencement of their life together in an idyllic Upstate New York town. That a fictional TV character could have a joyful, successful pregnancy and I couldn't struck me as brutally unjust. Before the credits rolled, I had slid off the couch and was sobbing face down on the living room carpet, tantrum style, while Patrick and Nora stared down at me from where they were perched on the recliner. When Patrick didn't rush to my side on the carpet, I wailed about how unfair it was that he paid more attention to the baby than to me.

More than anything, I wanted to get well again, but I wasn't the only one. my family and my doctors wanted me to get well more than anything too. They were literally working around the clock to take care of me, but I wasn't doing anything to take care of myself. No matter how much I wanted or needed them to, Patrick and my parents and Dr. Cook couldn't be solely responsible for getting me well. Ultimately, that responsibility lay within me. I refused to acknowledge that, though, and remained impatient and demanding.

Dr. Cook hadn't abandoned me, though. During the days I mistook for her radio silence, she was working on a plan. A new outpatient clinic had opened in Manhattan that focused solely on perinatal mood disorders. Each patient at The Clinic would be a mother who was suffering from mental illness, a mother like me, and each staff member would be a specialist in maternal mental health. There was a day care on-site. Nora would remain by my side or close by as I sat in my treatment sessions. This was what I had always wanted, Dr. Cook said. This was where I would get well. It was the care I had daydreamed I would receive when I first screamed for help that past winter. I just hoped that now, it wasn't too late.

Dr. Cook had secured a spot for me at The Clinic, and I would report there for intake the following morning. The day after that, my treatment would begin, and Nora would come with me. On that day, she would be one week old.

———

My mother came to pick me up and bring me to The Clinic the following morning. Patrick remained at home to take care of Nora—feeding her, swaddling her, switching on the tinkling nursery rhymes of the mobile that spun above her peaceful face as she slept. All the things I should have been doing but couldn't seem to manage. I shrugged on my army coat and quickly kissed Patrick and Nora goodbye.

My feeling of unreality was so severe by that point, that the only sensation I can liken it to is having taken a handful of hallucinogens and not being able to come down. The houses on my block became mocking faces; their small window eyes on the upper floors glared down at me, the wide windows on the bottom floor were a menacing smile. The colors of the cars parked along the sides of the street burned so bright they appeared to be at their melting point, hot to the touch. I could see the evil residing within each person who passed me, hollow eyes sagging inside sallow faces that taunted and judged. Unlike being in a state of psychosis, though, I didn't slip inside these delusions. I remained fully present, knowing what I was seeing wasn't real. Somehow, the knowing made things even more painful.

The outside world was terrifying, and I stopped trying to venture into it. I stayed inside, moving between our bed and the living room couch. Even the kitchen had become too frightening, the fluorescent bulb in the ceiling leaving me exposed and afraid. In the car on the way to The Clinic that morning, I put my head in my lap and my hands over my ears, willing the city to disappear.

———

The Clinic was beautiful. Located on the tenth floor of a Lexington Avenue high-rise, the space was all pale, wooden floors and exposed brick, glowing in the natural light that spilled in from the walls of windows. My mother and I sat on faux Eames chairs in the waiting room, and a receptionist placed a clipboard holding intake forms down on a gold accent table. Next to where the clipboard lay, a lone orchid sprouted from a clay pot.

I picked up the clipboard and glanced at it once before passing it to my mom. Words had become blurry, as had my ability to make sense of them. She filled out the intake forms for me. Psychiatrists and social workers came and introduced themselves to us. I wrapped my arms around my body, shrinking into the corner of the chair, my chin tucked into my collarbone. "Hi," I muttered, and weakly accepted their extended hands.

A social worker wanted to give my mother and me a tour of The Clinic—the airy yoga studio, the space filled with plush pillows and overstuffed chairs where we would hold our babies during group therapy, the nursery with polka-dot wallpaper and bright playmats, the dimly lit offices with copper colored leather couches and Moroccan rugs on the floor.

I refused to get up from my seat in the waiting room, wrapping my arms tighter around myself, like a terrified child on her first day of school. "That's okay," the social worker said, gently, "tomorrow." My mom went on the tour instead.

———

When I returned to the apartment, I found Patrick sitting at our dining room table, bouncing Nora in his lap. "Hi, Mommy," he said as Nora gurgled. As far gone as I was, I felt like she still knew me, that she was happy for my return. I took off my coat and reached for her, settling my face in the tender folds of her neck and kissing her ear. I was scared and skeptical, but I also still had a glint of faith. I would do the work, I would accept the help being offered to me at The Clinic, I would get stronger so I could be a good mom to my little girl.

My mom had brought over a green paper bag containing a box wrapped in ribbon. Inside the box were six cupcakes, each one frosted with a different color of thick pastel icing. She put the cupcakes on the table. It was April 5, my thirty-ninth birthday.

Chapter Thirteen

Patrick brought Nora and me to The Clinic each morning and came back at 2:00 to pick us up each afternoon. I was on maternity leave, but he had to balance being my caretaker with going to work, significantly cutting back his time at the museum to three or four hours a day. I didn't even consider this a sacrifice; I just expected it.

In the car on the way to the clinic, I tried not to cry or look out the window at the gray morning as we passed through the industrial landscape of Hunters Point on the way to the Midtown Tunnel. I stuck my index finger in Nora's tiny fist, and she gripped onto me, tight.

———

As soon as we entered The Clinic, I realized I had made a mistake. It was too clean, too bright, everyone's smiles too wide as they bent down to greet Nora, so small in her carrier. I looked up at Patrick. "I don't want to do this," I whispered. I started to cry. Patrick pulled down the brim of his baseball cap and shook his head, not looking at me. "We have no other choice," he said, staring straight forward. He was crying too. A blonde social worker smiled and made a gesture to follow her. I looked up at Patrick one last time, but he was already trailing her down the hall.

The social worker brought us to the nursery, where Nora would stay while I went to treatment. The walls were covered in wallpaper printed with thousands of tiny neon polka dots that throbbed angrily. The sugary voices of children singing lullabies piped in through speakers, loud and eerie. Bile rose in my throat.

The social worker looked at the three of us expectantly, but Patrick and I stood motionless, unable to speak. "Here," she said; "let's get you unpacked. Everyone's nervous the first day. It's okay! We're going to get you feeling better." She took our backpack from us and began setting up Nora's little bottles of formula on the pristine counter while an older woman with white-blonde hair cooed at our baby as she unbuckled her from the carrier, placing her gently on a playmat. Nora looked up at the mobile above her and kicked her legs. "She'll have a great time," the social worker said. "You can come with me; group will start in about fifteen minutes." I bent down to kiss Nora's fuzzy blonde head and squeezed Patrick's hand before I turned to follow the social worker. Patrick was right—I had no other choice.

———

The social worker's name was Olivia. She brought me into a large, airy room where six gray overstuffed rockers had been placed in a spacious semicircle facing a tidy wall of books arranged inside a built-in shelf. On the floor in the middle of the semicircle were overstuffed aquamarine footstools lit by a sliver of pale, cool light that had slipped in through the windows. The space was designed to soothe, but there was a buzzing growing louder inside me, telling me I had to get out of there immediately.

"I'm going to go check on the baby," I gasped.

"She's fine!" Olivia said. "You just left her!" She patted a rocker. "Here," she said; "get comfortable. You're a little early today; the other mommies will be here soon."

I tucked myself as far back in the chair as I could and wrapped my arms around myself tightly as I rocked back and forth.

———

There were three other mothers in the outpatient program the first two weeks I was at The Clinic, but two of them "graduated" soon after I arrived. I don't remember their names; they hardly interacted with me while we were in treatment together, seeming almost afraid of catching my illness if they got too close. The other mother was Alison, and, like me, she wasn't well enough to graduate for a long time. She had a three-month-old daughter named Callie who wore soft, giant bows wrapped around her bald head. Alison was the first mother I ever connected with, and we kept in touch for a long while after our time in the program together.

———

The first mother who came in was a pretty, voluptuous redhead with a close-cropped pixie cut. She plopped down in one of the rockers across from me.

"Hey! Welcome!" she said. "Oh, my god. You don't even know how amazing this program is. I was a mess when I got here. But now? I am so much better."

"Really?" I asked, weakly. "How long have you been here?"

"Two weeks. This is my last week. Before I graduate." I flashed back to Dr. Abrams's promise about the magical three-week recovery mark.

She picked up a chubby baby with a shock of curly blonde hair on his head out of the sleek stroller parked beside her chair. "Jesus, the subway was *so* crowded this morning! It's why we're late," she said, pulling up her T-shirt and unbuckling her bra. "They put me on Zoloft, so it's totally safe for me to feed him," she said with a shrug as the baby latched onto her full breast.

The mother who came in next was soft-spoken and petite, with dark hair grazing her shoulders. She wore a printed dress with black tights and ballet flats. "Hi," she said. "You're going to love it here so much. I came here after a week in the hospital. They found out I'm bipolar," she whispered. "But they switched my medication and now I'm healing. They're so good here."

I nodded like I understood, but the women were making me feel more disoriented. They seemed so at ease with themselves, so at ease in The Clinic. Why were they here? I didn't know if their stories should give me hope or if I should feel weak with the defeat of knowing I was so far away from being well.

———

Alison was the last to arrive. She raised her hand to me in a small wave as she sat down. Her long hair was still wet, and, like me, she wore baggy sweatpants and sneakers. She sat back and folded her arms across her chest. I noticed that, also like me, her dark eyes darted like a trapped animal around the room.

———

Olivia came back into the room and began group therapy with check-ins. We went around the circle, and each mother shared what was going on in her life at the moment. The mother with the short red hair was upset because her husband's work schedule had forced her to cancel her girls' night. The mother wearing ballet flats was a little apprehensive because she was hosting a Passover Seder at her apartment over the weekend. I felt smacked with bewilderment and anger. What was I doing here? How did these women have social plans when I couldn't even go outside without covering my eyes? The buzzing inside me grew louder, shaking me with its vibration until I could no longer sit still.

I pushed myself out of the chair and, like I had done in the hospital, fled from the room, beginning to pace. I was in a cage—inside my mind, inside my body, inside the group therapy session with these mothers who seemed like they were fine.

The Clinic was laid out in a rectangle, with the nursery and an art therapy studio at the center and offices lining the outer hallways. I walked the loop quickly, the brick walls pulsing. Each time I passed the nursery, I lingered for a moment in the doorway, looking in on Nora.

Even in my disconcerted state, I could sense my pacing was out of place in The Clinic, which was more comparable to an upscale spa than a psychiatric hospital. I knew I needed to calm down, but I had no idea how to do it. The staff let me go for a little while, until eventually Olivia found me. "You seem a little agitated," she said, touching my elbow. "Why don't we go into my office?"

Inside, Olivia's office was plant filled and calm, but outside the office window, the skyscrapers seemed to bend and twist into surreal shapes, like an M. C. Escher print. I tried to keep my focus on Olivia's face.

"Have you ever tried CBT?" she asked. She pulled out a notebook. "It's cognitive behavioral therapy. We're going to be working on read-justing some of your behavioral patterns and giving you some coping strategies for when you feel stressed."

I took the notebook from her and began to flip through. It was filled with charts and acronyms, like a handbook for someone who had just taken a job in middle management at a marketing firm. I nodded and passed the notebook back.

In our session, Olivia taught me that when I was feeling anxious, I could close my eyes and take deep breaths while pretending to brush negative thoughts away by repeating a vigorous downward brushing motion with my hands. She modeled the motion and then made me try it on my own.

"Feel better?" she asked, cocking her head brightly.

"Yeah," I lied. "That felt better."

"When you're at home and you feel anxious, you can grab some ice cubes and just close your eyes and squeeze. It's going to feel really cold, but it's another technique that will help ground you."

"Okay," I said, my voice shaky with resignation. "Okay, I'll try that." I knew that I never would.

———

After our therapy session, lunch arrived. Each morning, patients were presented with a menu from an upscale midtown sandwich shop, and we could order anything we wanted. I had missed ordering that morning, but the receptionist selected a grilled chicken sandwich on whole grain bread with sprouts and avocado and left it for me in its plastic case on a table in the art studio. The two mothers from earlier that morning sat at the table across from each other, eating, laughing, and scrolling through their phones like it was just a regular afternoon. I left my sandwich on the table, untouched.

———

Like the structure of the days at the hospital, the remainder of the afternoon was filled with back-to-back activities: yoga, art therapy, music class. I sat on the sidelines for each one, unable to bring myself to participate as the other mothers flowed through sun salutations, decoupaged covers for the baby books they were crafting, and shook tiny maracas to the beat of sweet nursery rhymes they would teach to their babies.

The music teacher had gray braids that reached her soft hips and wore Birkenstocks with thick, woolly socks. At the end of class, she asked each mother to share a "moment of wonder" they had experienced with their baby in the past week. I went last.

I was sitting against the wall, away from the class, with my knees pulled up to my chest.

"A moment of wonder?" I took a breath. "Okay. Well, um, my daughter was born this week. And I guess a moment of wonder for me was when the doctor handed her to me and she just opened her eyes and looked at me and started reaching for my face..." My voice broke and I covered my face with my hands, my shoulders shaking. I was crying so hard I didn't make a sound.

———

Patrick came back at 2:30 to pick us up. He didn't ask me how the day went; he could see it in my red and ragged face. The day-care teacher helped us get Nora strapped into her carrier.

"Look at her," the teacher said once Nora was buckled in. "She's just perfect. Ten tiny fingers, ten tiny toes, and she's all yours!" She looked at us, beaming.

The teacher was right; Nora was perfect. She was preternaturally easy, crying only when she was hungry, sleeping easily, tucking her head into the nook between my neck and my shoulder. She craned her head, so alert from where she lay in her carrier, her navy eyes open wide, her lips puckered into a tiny overbite. She looked like a little fledgling sparrow. My perfect baby. And I was locked inside my cage, unable to enjoy any of it.

———

When we arrived back at the apartment, I took a few Ativan and lay down. I was exhausted, my body wrung out. As I drifted off, I ticked through the ways I could make myself disappear: heavy backpacks and rivers, ten minutes of holding my head down in the bathtub, the bottle of bleach under the sink. As the medication pulled its dark blanket over my eyes, a new thought floated past: the rows of prescription bottles lining the medicine cabinet. Swallowing handfuls of tiny pills while Patrick and Nora slept.

———

The combination of benzodiazepines and Seroquel I took in the evenings made it easy for me to fall asleep at night, but I would always awaken at dawn, paralyzed by the weight of knowing I had to make it through another day. Next to the bed where I lay, staring at the ceiling, Nora's mobile spun above her bassinet—tiny stuffed zoo animals marching slowly in circles to the tinkling sound of Elvis Presley's "Teddy Bear" being played on chimes. In those early-morning hours, I felt like I knew the true meaning of grief.

———

In the car on the way to The Clinic, I watched Nora's eyes grow large in the darkness of the Midtown Tunnel. She was so new yet already so in awe of the world. In the early months of her life, my mother would say, "She really wanted to be here"—a double-edged observation that was both a dig at my illness and a truth. These hurtful comments were typical for her at the time.

My mother was already pulling away from Patrick and me in those first few weeks, making it clear that she had her own life and was planning to continue living it. She frequently invoked my sister-in-law Celine's mom, who had come over to cook and clean and care for my niece Zoe when Celine was unwell. My mother firmly let us know this would not be her.

Depending on my mom for childcare was not an option. She told Patrick and me repeatedly that the three of us were our own unit now, that we needed to figure out how to manage.

My parents only lived an hour away, but each time we asked for help, my mom came up with excuses: She needed to take the car in for inspection, she had lunch plans, my father wanted her to help with some paperwork, the cleaning service was coming.

We frequently asked her to pick me up from The Clinic and keep me company for the few hours before Patrick arrived home so that he could work a full day. When she did come, she loudly made it known that she had been inconvenienced. She complained about the traffic, the expensive parking, the late hour she would arrive home to cook my father dinner.

Patrick was often furious with her. He couldn't understand why she couldn't help when we were so clearly struggling—she didn't work and lived so close. I vacillated in my feelings. No matter how much my mother complained, I loved the feeling of being able to sit next to her on the couch at the end of the day, exhausted from the hours at The Clinic. She held Nora, who clung to her, snoring gently with her cheek resting on my mother's chest.

At some level, I knew my mother's complaints and avoidance were her way of protecting herself from seeing her daughter in so much pain. And she was furious too, at the illness that had taken hold of me. The illness lived inside of me, though, and she couldn't separate us.

On one of our afternoons together on the couch, my mom looked at me and said, "Sweetie, if I could just take the sickness out of your *keppe* and put it in my own, I would, my love, I would."

My mother, my doctors, the social worker, the patients who were so quickly getting well—everyone was just doing the best they could.

———

On my second day at The Clinic, I fought against my urges to scream, to cry, to run out of the room, to frantically pace. I let myself be led through the morning group activities like an obedient child. I lasted until my individual therapy session with Olivia.

She opened the session by asking me to describe my morning routine and my feelings associated with each step. I wasn't sure what she was expecting to hear, but she was visibly shaken when I told her the truth.

I have an unsettling habit of smiling or laughing when I have to express a deeply painful thought during therapy sessions. That morning with Olivia, I responded to her with a vacant giggle.

"My morning routine?" I asked, an eerie grin on my face. "Well, I wake up usually at dawn. And then I lie in bed, and I usually think about how much I want to die."

Olivia's face went slack. "What do you mean you think about how you want to die?" Gone was her usual friendliness.

"I mean, I think about how much I don't want to be here. How much I want to escape from feeling this way. How much I'm failing as Nora's mother. And I think about all the ways I can disappear."

"Barrie," she replied, putting her papers down and staring at me. "Barrie, this is serious. We take suicidality very seriously here. We need to talk about this. Hold on." She picked up her office phone and dialed quickly. "Hi," she said. "I have Barrie in here? Can we come in for a few minutes?"

Olivia brought me into a spacious office down the hall, full of light and plants and a large glass coffee table with art books on it. I sat down on the dark, leather couch. On a bookshelf I spotted Brooke Shields's *Down Came the Rain*.

A tall woman with an expensive-looking haircut came out from behind a large wooden desk to greet me. She wore pointy heels, and a tiny diamond glittered in the hollow of her throat. Like the previous reproductive psychiatrist we had seen, the doctor's demeanor was no-nonsense, and sleek. "Hi. Dr. Weissman, director of The Clinic. Want to tell me what's been going on?"

As though she was tattling on a petulant child, Olivia immediately began speaking for me. I didn't mind; I was just so grateful that I didn't have to repeat my story again.

Despite my anguish, the glimmer of hope had begun to flicker again as I sat in Dr. Weissman's office. *This might be it.* Dr. Weissman was the director of a clinic specializing in perinatal mood disorders. She might be the one to finally solve my problem.

When Olivia finished, Dr. Weissman spoke. "First, you're going to call your husband and tell him to come here. Then we're going to talk about some options for you."

I felt flooded with relief. There were options. This doctor knew what she was doing.

Patrick arrived quickly. "I took a car here," he said. "What's going on?"

The doctor relayed to Patrick what I had told Olivia in our session. Then she looked at me. "As Olivia said, we take suicidality very seriously here. So I'm going to recommend hospitalization."

Patrick turned to me. "Why do you keep telling people that you want to hurt yourself?" Then he turned back to Dr. Weissman. "Absolutely not. There is no way she is going to be hospitalized. She was already hospitalized once, and it made her worse. It set us way back. She's not going again. Not a chance."

"This time, we would recommend that she be hospitalized at a hospital closer to here—on the Upper East Side. It would be a much different experience than her previous stay. The care there is superior. And there would be more patients—well, there would be more patients you might feel comfortable around. A different, uh, different clientele. More like here at The Clinic."

Patrick and I knew what she meant by this. We didn't know how expensive The Clinic was or if my insurance was covering part of it, but what we did know was that on the morning I passed off the intake papers to my mom, we assumed she had signed off on footing whatever bill needed to be paid. We were lucky that way.

With the gourmet sandwiches, the yoga and art studios, the specialist teachers who came to teach baby music and movement classes, there was no way the care at The Clinic could have been cheap. In the months I was in treatment there, not one staff member or patient of color passed through The Clinic's glass doors. And even Alison and I, who were probably the least put together of all the patients, still wore leggings and sweatpants with tiny name-brand insignias on them. Did being in treatment at a center where everyone looked the same as me make me feel more comfortable? It is a question I still have a difficult time grappling with—the answer too embarrassing to confess if it's true.

In Dr. Weissman's office that morning, Patrick remained firm. "No," he said. "What are the other options?"

"We're going to put her on a new medication, Zyprexa," Dr. Weissman said, looking at me. "You're up here," she said, making a motion with her hand. "We need to bring you down here." She pushed her palm toward the floor.

"What does Zyprexa do?" I asked, my voice small.

Dr. Weissman faced both of us and sighed. "It's an antipsychotic."

"Do I have postpartum psychosis?" I asked.

"We can't be sure yet," Dr. Weissman said. "But we're going to give this a try."

She looked at Patrick. "This medication is heavy," she said. "You're going to need to watch her all weekend. You're turning your home into a makeshift hospital."

The plan was to have me get in bed as soon as I got home and take the Zyprexa. Patrick would be by my side, watching me for signs of dizziness, a rapid or slowed heartbeat, slurring speech. My mom would come and stay the night, watching the baby as Patrick watched over me. I was free of all responsibilities. All I had to do was take the medication and wait. Doctor's orders.

Unbelievably, the idea that I might have postpartum psychosis filled me with a deep sense of comfort. Finally, we were getting to the bottom of this. My disorder had a treatment. It had a name.

At home, I lined up my medication: Zoloft, Seroquel, Ativan, Ambien, and now Zyprexa. *Here we go!* I thought as I took the pills. I waited. I went to sleep. I woke up. I took the pills again. I repeated this all weekend, but nothing happened. Nothing changed. By Sunday night I still felt exactly the same.

Chapter Fourteen

On Monday, back at The Clinic, Dr. Weissman took me off the Zyprexa.

"If it's not doing anything, it's not worth it," she said.

"So, then, I don't have postpartum psychosis?" I asked.

"No," she replied. "No, that would be highly unlikely at this point."

"Then what do I have?" I asked. My tone was pleading.

"We're still not sure," she said. "But you're going to hang out with us here for a few weeks."

"A few weeks, like three?" I asked.

"We'll see," she said. "But you're going to try. And you're going to get better."

Throughout my treatment I heard those words—*You're going to get better*—hundreds of times. *How?* I thought. *When?* But no one ever had an answer.

———

On the ride through the Midtown Tunnel that morning, Patrick's and my mother's words from the other day ran through my head: *We have no other choice.* I would have to fight through the agonizing discomfort of being trapped inside my mind, and I would have to try.

———

In those next few weeks at The Clinic, I left Nora in the day-care room less and less. I held her during group therapy sessions and fed her miniature bottles of formula, the weight of her and rhythm of her breathing grounding me. "She's my therapy," I told the group. And they reassured me. "You're such a good mommy," Alison said. "You're so patient and gentle."

I still felt encased by the sticky web that kept me in my suspended state of unreality, but the more I tried, the more I held Nora and fed her and put her down for her naps, the more I could feel the leaden weight of depression lift, just the slightest bit. I smiled a little more; I cracked a few jokes. The jokes were always self-deprecating, but still, there were brief flashes of my sense of humor that had been deadened for so many months, replaced by the robotic loops of questions asked in the choked, little-girl voice.

During that week, the two mothers from the week before departed and a new patient arrived: Kara. Kara was a fashion stylist who lived in Williamsburg. Long and lanky, she walked through the halls of The Clinic leading with her hipbones. Each day, she wore the same outfit: a gray sweatshirt, Levi's, and Birkenstocks, her artfully bleached hair piled in a lazy bun atop her head like a messy crown.

I realized later that the extreme thinness, the mussed hair, and the same outfit every day was because she was wading through a long and unrelenting postpartum depression; but to me, it just made her look impossibly cool.

The first morning Kara arrived, I felt threatened, as though she was someone from my former, carefree life in North Brooklyn who had arrived to infiltrate The Clinic and judge me, but I quickly came to like her. She began bringing me little toys her son had outgrown to pass down to Nora. Her son was nearly a year old. She had been suffering for a long time.

It felt safe, just the three of us. Kara was open about her depression, and Alison spoke about her debilitating anxiety. She couldn't get a handle on the thoughts racing through her mind that something was wrong with Callie—she called her pediatrician every day with a new imagined symptom. Alison knew intellectually that she was acting irrationally, but she couldn't control her compulsions. She worried she would never be able to return to work at the hospital where she worked as a psychiatrist.

I tried to describe my feeling of unreality, the places I knew by heart seeming unfamiliar, the people who appeared as body doubles of themselves. Alison and Kara would shake their heads. "That sounds awful," they would say, looking at the ground. As much as I could trust them, my own unidentifiable illness still made me feel so alone.

After having ruled out postpartum psychosis, Dr. Weissman and Olivia began to echo the same diagnosis that had been given to me by Dr. Cook and Dr. Abrams: I had major depressive disorder, and my depersonalization and derealization were symptoms.

"But it never goes away," I would tell them. "I feel like this all the time."

"It's going to," they would reply.

"When?" I would ask.

"Soon," they would say. "It will go away soon."

I still cried every day—in group therapy, in individual therapy, in art therapy, in yoga class. But I felt myself trying. And the doctors felt it too. They seemed to take me more seriously—I never had to lay eyes on a CBT notebook again.

———

After my long days of "trying" at The Clinic, though, I emotionally deteriorated at home. Dr. Weissman and Olivia suggested that I try commuting to The Clinic on my own. That way, I could start gaining some independence in taking care of Nora, and Patrick would be able to work full days. Although our lives were far from back to normal at that point, the idea was that the more we went through the motions, the more quickly we might be able to will the normalcy to return.

In the car rides home from the clinic, I felt safe inside the cocoon of tinted windows and air-conditioning, the familiar pop songs drifting through on the radio. Once I got home, though, I started sobbing, hard, usually while I held Nora in my arms.

It wasn't that I didn't want to take care of Nora—I did. I wanted to be good at taking care of her with a fierceness that felt almost feral. But any confidence I had ever felt in myself had been stripped bare. I felt like I was back to the clumsy, chubby child who had been teased on the playground, my hands like fumbling butterfingers.

There is a video taken of me during that month; I'm giving Nora a bath in the kitchen sink. You can hear me speaking in a singsong voice: "Nora Madeline, it's your bath time!" My voice sounds high-pitched—and frightened. You can see Patrick's outstretched hands right over the sink, ready, just in case I slipped.

———

When you are mentally ill, you become so fragile that the slightest shift in the atmosphere can cause you to shatter. In my third week at The Clinic, things changed, and any progress I had begun to build splintered.

First, Kara graduated. As much as I appreciated her presence, her quick recovery hit me with a bitter blow of jealousy. Also, Alison was gone. When I asked where she was, Olivia told me she had gone away for a little while, that she might be back in a couple of weeks. That was all the information I got. In Kara's and Alison's places were new mothers, women I didn't have the emotional wherewithal to get to know. In group and at lunchtime, I once again fell silent, wrapping my arms tightly around my middle.

———

On Thursday of that week, we had my friend Amy come over in the afternoon. She was a close friend—she had hosted my baby shower—and wanted to meet Nora. None of our friends had met the baby yet; I was far too ashamed of myself to let anyone except our immediate family near me. Amy knew I was suffering, and I had told her about my fears of having DPDR.

Amy arrived at our apartment with gifts for Nora, hand-me-down clothing from her own toddler daughter, and gifts for me: homemade soaps, household cleaning products made with apple cider vinegar.

She sat down on our couch and held Nora, wrapping her in a blanket knit by one of Patrick's aunts. "I haven't held a newborn in so long!" she crowed. She bounced Nora rhythmically in her arms, and Nora immediately fell sound asleep. I felt envious of Amy's confidence with my little girl.

"How are you feeling?" Amy asked.

"I think I feel a little better. I do."

"Oh, good," Amy said. "Because I was researching DPDR, and it said that once you have it, it never goes away. I was really worried. Like worried that you were going to have to be institutionalized forever or something. Glad you're feeling better," she said, bending her face down to coo at Nora.

This comment broke me—it seemed so cruel. And it also seemed like it might be true. I wasn't really better. This was going to be my life. Terror flowed through my body like melting ice.

———

Over the previous weeks, the plans I had to make myself disappear were still present but had dimmed. That night in bed, though, the voices announcing each plan marched through my mind, and they were blaringly loud. They shouted the same simple message over and over: *"Do it."*

Even with the medication, I couldn't sleep that night. I lay still with my eyes closed as I heard Patrick get up every two hours to feed Nora. I still didn't help with the feedings, because all the doctors agreed that I needed to rest as much as possible. Patrick was constantly exhausted from this sacrifice.

At around 4:00 a.m. I reached over to Patrick and shook his shoulder. He was facing away from me in our bed, deep inside one of his few precious hours of sleep. "Babe," I said, shaking him. "Babe. I'm so scared." Patrick stirred a bit and rolled over to face me. He opened his eyes to slits and said the two words that shattered the final shards left of me: "Shut. Up." And he rolled over, his measured breathing telling me he had fallen back into a heavy sleep. In his unconscious state, he had revealed his true feelings.

I got up and went on the couch. All the signs this week had led me to this point, and Patrick's words had confirmed it: No one wanted me here anymore. Even my parents were gone—away for ten days for a family friend's wedding in Napa, where they had been joined by Zach and Celine.

The message was clear: Everyone was ready to move on with their lives, without me. I thought of all the bottles in the medicine cabinet. It would be so simple. I would be gone. And they could be free.

I went to get Nora from her bassinet and brought her to the couch. She slept on top of me, and I rubbed her little legs, already growing plump. She would never remember, I thought. She would never have to live with a crazy mom.

At around 5:00 a.m. I put her back in her bassinet, kissing the top of her warm head as I lay her down, covering her with the knit blanket. She would be waking up soon for her bottle. I didn't have a lot of time. I didn't kiss Patrick, scared I would wake him before I did what I needed to do.

I went into the bathroom and opened the medicine cabinet, removing the orange bottles and lining them up, one by one, on the vanity. I glanced over the labels quickly. I would take the Zyprexa, the Seroquel, skip the Zoloft. All of the Ativan and Klonopin. Last, I would take the fourteen Ambien I had left. That way, I would fall asleep before I realized what I had done.

My hands shaking, I opened each bottle and turned on the tap, grabbing handfuls of pills and quickly washing them down with the water I sipped from the cup of my palm. It didn't take longer than five minutes to consume nearly sixty pills.

I left the bottles on the counter, turned off the tap, and walked quickly back to the living room, adrenaline making my blood pound so hard I could feel it in my teeth. I lay on my back and covered myself with a blanket, closing my eyes. My pulse began to slow. I let myself drift. I let myself feel the web untangle, the moment of relief before I passed out.

———

That day, time moved in flashes, and I would briefly emerge before sinking back under. The scuff of the EMTs' boots on the wooden floors of our apartment. The jangle of a police officer's key ring. The bump of the stretcher being loaded into the ambulance. The beep of the monitors in the ER. The warm mitt of Patrick's hand in mine as he stood next to the gurney where I lay. Patrick's faraway voice asking if I please might have some more blankets; I was shivering. The hollow tunnel of an MRI machine. The soft hands of a nurse as she changed me into pajamas. The comforting, bright red glow of the Pepsi-Cola sign across the East River outside my window. Patrick's gentle kiss goodbye. The scratchy cotton pillowcase on my cheek.

I knew I hadn't succeeded, but I could have stayed submerged in the inky darkness I kept slipping back into forever. For the first time in almost a year, I remembered what it felt like to be at peace.

Patrick and I never discussed what happened during those lost hours until many years later. All I knew was that the day had begun at dawn and ended sometime deep into the night.

Chapter Fifteen

I woke up alone in a spacious room with a huge window overlooking the East River. The container ships glided slowly down the waterway, and the river dazzled and glittered in the sunrise. I was still groggy, but I could tell that the day hadn't yet begun. There were no sounds in the halls signaling that the ward had awakened. As I did each morning, I checked to see if my world had returned to normal, but my mind was still so thickly padded that I couldn't tell.

I took in the room. I was lying on one of two wooden twin beds. I had no roommate yet, but there was sure to be someone soon. I would revel in the solitude for as long as I could. There were two wooden nightstands with a lamp. Like at a hotel, a notepad and fine-tipped marker lay atop the small stand under a reading lamp. Next to the notepad was a toiletry bag filled with miniature toothpaste, a travel toothbrush in a plastic pouch, and sample-sized bottles of shampoo, conditioner, and bodywash. Imprinted on the toiletry bag were the letters "NYE": New York East. Patrick had taken Dr. Weissman's suggestion.

On the far-facing wall were two armoires, separated by a large desk. I slowly unwrapped the blankets and pushed myself out of bed, feeling lightheaded for a moment as I stood. I made my way over to the armoire and opened it, finding two towels folded neatly, a washcloth, and, mercifully, my black leggings and favorite blue T-shirt. On top of my clothes lay a pair of dark green slipper socks with white treading on the bottom.

I took the two towels and toiletry bag into the bathroom, avoiding looking at myself in the plastic sheet mirror above the sink. I turned on the shower. Like in the other psych ward, the bathroom door didn't lock. But the shower curtain wasn't moldy, and the water ran hot.

———

I dressed in my soft, clean clothes, feeling a weak relief, like I had just emerged from a long bout of the flu, the fever finally burned off. I noticed two books on the large desk and went to pick them up. Whoever had stayed in the room before me had excellent taste. They had left two of my favorites: a book of short stories by Katherine Heiny and an infamous memoir by Cat Marnell, where she spends two weeks in the very same ward. I took the books and lay back down in my twin bed. It was still difficult to concentrate on reading, but I was able to flip through both books, finding comfort in rereading my favorite passages.

Those early-morning minutes were full of an incongruous sense of peace. I didn't think about the day before; I didn't think about what lay ahead. It was a small respite, an hour where I lay with my books, still cloaked in the hangover from the pills. I selfishly treasured the time. It didn't last long. The rhythmic squeak of nurses' shoes making their rounds through the tiled halls and the clatter of breakfast trays being wheeled in announced the start of a new day. And I was hit with the full force of what I had done.

———

The first weekend in the ward at New York East is hazy, but I do remember running to the phones as soon as the jigsaw of memories from the day before locked into place.

I had almost abandoned my husband and baby, and their absence that morning ripped through me with an overwhelming ferocity. *What have I done?* The words rang and reverberated clearly in my mind.

———

The rules at New York East, or 11 East, as I soon learned the ward there was referred to, were much more relaxed. Phones turned on early and turned off late. There was a large bank of them, all in a row, with an overstuffed leather bench to sit on, like you would find at an old-fashioned diner. Still, the phones faced out, toward the nurses' station. In every psych ward, the patients are being watched.

No phone cards were necessary, and Patrick picked up after the first ring.

"Babe," I said. "Babe, I'm so sorry. I'm so sorry. I didn't mean to do this. I won't do it again, I promise. I promise I won't leave you and Nora. I'm going to get better, I promise. I didn't want to die. I just wanted to escape. I needed to just disappear for a while. I never wanted to leave." As I said these words, they felt true. Like the patients I had envied before, the ones who were lost in their delusions or shot up into oblivion with liquid tranquilizers, I was just desperate, for a few hours, to feel free.

"It's okay, sweetie, it's okay," Patrick replied. "No one is mad at you. We were just so worried. No one is blaming you. We know you're so sick, honey. We just want you to get well."

"Did you talk to anyone?" I asked. "Do you know how long I'm going to be here?"

"I did," he said. "They said you're going to be here for at least ten days." Patrick sighed.

"Ten days?" I asked. "Are you serious? What am I supposed to do for ten days? How am I going to see Nora?" I gave myself full permission at that point to give in, and I began to sob. If I was going to be in the ward for over a week, anyway, I didn't care who saw my public display of despair. *Let them write about it on their damn clipboards*, I thought.

"Deep breaths, hon," Patrick said. "Visiting hours are from 11 to 7 every day. I'll be there right at 11. I'll be with you all day." Patrick didn't say then what he was thinking: *Ten days? You were about to disappear for the rest of our lives.*

"What about Nora?" I asked. "Who is watching her?"

"My parents came up," Patrick said. "She'll be with them. Then we can figure out when I can bring her to see you."

"What about my parents?" I asked. "Have you spoken with them?"

"Yeah. Yeah, I did," Patrick replied. "They said they're going to stay in California. They're going to stay for the wedding. They'll see you when they get back."

I was silent for a moment as I took this in. I don't think my family enjoyed the rest of their vacation knowing that I was hospitalized, but their priority had been chosen, and it wasn't me.

"Okay," I said, breathing heavily. "Okay." I swiped the back of my hand over my eyes. "How's the baby?" I asked, my voice cracking open into a quiet howl.

"She's good, honey. She misses her mommy. She's going to see you soon. Listen, I'll be there in a few hours, okay? I'll be with you all day."

"Okay," I said, still breathing hard. "I'll see you soon."

"Just try to hang in there, hon," Patrick said. "I love you so much."

"I love you so much, too." I hung up the receiver, not getting up from the bench.

There was so much information in our brief conversation: Would Patrick's parents now be held up as saviors, while mine continued to stay as far away as possible? What would I owe them for this? I was awash in a fresh wave of humiliation. I knew this was far afield from anything they could have ever expected from me as a wife, from me as a mother.

For my in-laws, the words "I love you" were rarely uttered. Not that they weren't loving—like Patrick, they projected a gentle, unwavering stability. But displays of emotion seemed too bold, too brash for their quiet sensibilities.

What, then, could they possibly think of who their son had married? I felt like I would be trapped in the spotlight of their silent judgment for a long time to come.

And did everyone really forgive me? For a long time after my attempt at escaping the world, I believed it was true, that I had been absolved. The sins of the sick are always forgiven, aren't they?

I would eventually learn that Patrick lived in a quiet, paralyzing fear for years. He didn't believe that this would be my only attempt at taking my life. He believed we were beginning a pattern that I would be doomed to repeat for years to come. Yes, I was forgiven for my actions, but it was hard for him to forgive me for how my actions had left him irrevocably changed.

———

Ten days. This time, I promised myself, I would be honest. This time, we would finally get it right. Ten days was enough time to figure out what was wrong with me, wasn't it?

———

I drifted through the morning hours before Patrick's visit. Nothing had changed; I was still chained inside the same glass box from which I viewed the world through its dirty panes, looking out onto my contorted unreality. Gone was my usual impulse to pace, though; whatever medication I had ingested the day before had coated my body and mind in a dense layer of cotton wool.

I ate breakfast at a table alone, looking down at the joggers and cyclists and couples holding hands as they made their way down the waterfront path, tiny dolls from where I sat at the window on the eleventh floor. Their distance made things easier. I could pretend they weren't real, that life wasn't going on without me.

The activities for the day were posted on a neon-lit board: chair yoga class at 10:00 a.m. announced in bright red lights like it was the new blockbuster movie. The activities at 11 East were abundant and occurred nonstop throughout the day. There was yoga, dance therapy, pet therapy, creative writing, meditation, watercolor painting, complete with easels in an art studio flooded with natural light. Saturday and Sunday were ice-cream social days, and patients could enjoy sundaes stopped with whipped cream and maraschino cherries while watching the barges float slowly down the river.

While I waited for visiting hours that first morning, I chose what would become my favorite activity: grooming, where I could spend a quiet hour in the art studio painting glittery designs on my nails.

Patrick and I later joked that had I been feeling better, I probably would have loved my stay at 11 East. It was like a cruise ship, but without the fresh air.

I wasn't feeling well, though. My jittery pacing compulsion was missing, but in its place was a heavy resignation. I wept constantly. I seemed physically unable to stop. In the notes from my first few interviews with doctors and social workers, they wrote, *unable to complete interview due to excessive tearfulness.* When the doctors commented on my excessive crying, citing my "poor coping skills," I would apologize. "I'm sorry," I would say, "but I have a five-week-old baby at home. I'm sick and I'm trying everything, but nothing is making me better and no one is helping me. Wouldn't you be crying too?" I always wondered about the doctors' accusations of my visible sadness. Should I have been stoic? Happy? Wasn't it more appropriate to be sad?

At the hospital, Patrick spent a lot of time just quietly holding me. There was a patient there, a sweet boy no older than twenty, who passed each day playing Uno with his worried parents. He brought me box after box of tissues. I was so sad and frustrated. I was so exhausted.

The first day Patrick came to visit me, a student string quartet played for the patients. They were earnest, and the music was beautiful. Patrick and I sat on folding chairs to watch, leaning heavily into one another, the music opening a raw ache inside us both. He was wearing my favorite threadbare black T-shirt. Outside, the weather had become warm. It was fully spring.

Chapter Sixteen

When I went to sleep that first night, the other twin bed in my room had been empty, but when I awoke on the second morning, I saw a figure humped beneath the white cotton blankets. I was nervous. It didn't appear that seventy-two-hour holds were an option at 11 East; most people stayed for at least a week, usually longer. This strange lump under the covers and I would be sharing a living space for a while.

After about ten minutes, the lump rose, stretching her arms into a large V above her head, letting out a satisfied yawn. A short crop of dark hair shot up in all different directions. She yawned again and lay back down.

"Hey," she said softly, her head resting on her pillow. "I'm Sam."

"Hi," I replied. "Barrie. Did you get here last night?"

"Yeah. You were sound asleep. I'm glad I didn't wake you."

"Yeah," I said. "They upped my medication, and it just knocks me out. I also have a five-week-old daughter at home, so I'm just exhausted all the time anyway."

"Aww," Sam said. "Five weeks? Oh, man. You have postpartum depression?"

"Something like that," I replied.

"Oh, you poor thing. My sister had that too. Did you try to hurt yourself?" she asked, lowering her voice.

"Yeah," I said. "I did. I took a bunch of pills. It didn't do anything, though." I gave a short laugh. "I think it just made me take a long nap."

"Ha," she said. "That's why I'm here too. I took a bottle of Klonopin. Didn't do shit."

We both laughed a little.

"Why did you do it?" I asked.

"Ehh, fight with my girlfriend. My mom was bugging me. I don't know. I don't think I really wanted to die—just, like, get away from it all, you know?"

"Yeah," I replied. "I don't think I really wanted to die either. Did your sister get better?" I asked.

"She did. Her daughter is four, and she's the best mom. And you know what? I can already tell. You're gonna get better and be the best mommy too. What's your daughter's name?"

"Nora," I said, smiling. "Her name is Nora."

I still checked if the world had returned to normal that morning. It still hadn't. But what had changed was that in those moments of connecting with Sam, I remembered what it was like to feel comfort. I remembered what it might be like to feel the pleasure of friendship again, to feel that sweet form of love.

Sam was young, in her mid-twenties. She wore her hair shaved on one side and the other side flopped over her left eye, like a '90s skater. She seemed to have an endless supply of sweatpants, which she wore with one leg pulled up, revealing tube socks and Adidas soccer sandals. To keep her breasts flattened beneath her T-shirt, she put on three sports bras every morning.

Sam was born and raised in Astoria, where she still lived with her huge Greek family. She spoke with a heavy Queens accent, her gravelly voice projecting the loving warmth of a housedress-wearing, cookie-baking grandmother. I was still miserable, but Sam made me feel safe, and I followed her around the ward like a stray kitten until she was released, ten days later.

———

On the weekends, the usual team of doctors and nurses clears out and the ward is hushed and deserted. Since I had arrived on a Friday night, I wouldn't meet with the team who would follow my case until Monday.

Instead, I had check-ins with young residents and interns, none of whom I ever saw again. One resident unhelpfully suggested to Patrick and me that if I didn't begin to recover from my depressive state soon, the next step for me would most likely be ECT—electroconvulsive therapy. We knew nothing about the therapy and imagined leather straps wrapped around my head and biting on pieces of wood as my personality became more and more erased until there was nothing left of me but the shell of my body.

Doctors, nurses, and social workers often seemed to feel justified in carelessly tossing out advice and diagnoses without any regard for how much it might frighten—or damage—us.

———

On Monday morning, the mood on the ward snapped out of the drowsy, dreamlike state of the weekend. I hadn't noticed, but there were speakers on the wall behind each bed, and at 7:00 a.m. sharp, a man's voice boomed a cheerful wake-up call. His announcement that "all patients should please report to the lobby for a vitals check" made him sound like he was the director of a demented summer camp.

When I woke up, I no longer thought about how I wanted to die. But every day, I was greeted by the crushing nausea of guilt. I missed Nora and I was missing Nora—the days I was in the hospital were days with her that I would never get back. I tried to remember how she felt—her weight, her skin, her breath—but it was too hard, and I gave up easily.

Each day there began the same way that first week: I woke up, got my vitals checked, showered, dressed, and then ran to the phones to call Patrick. I sobbed incomprehensibly into the receiver, repeating how sorry I was and how much I missed him and Nora, even though I would see him in just a few short hours.

There was a staticky buzz of anticipation among the patients that Monday morning as the team started to arrive, just before breakfast. They were a large group—much larger than the team at the first psych ward—but the ward at 11 East also had double the number of patients. They still filed in briskly, clipboards in hand, but they seemed more approachable; their postures were relaxed, and some smiled as they greeted their patients. Most of the doctors and nurses and social workers were young, but there were a handful who looked like they were seasoned pros. I felt that familiar faint tinge of optimism as I regarded the group through a film of tears while I wept to Patrick on the telephone.

After I hung up with Patrick, a woman in her early twenties approached me where I sat red-eyed and shoulder-slumped on the bench in front of the phones. My vision was blurry. but as she approached, I did a double take. She looked like a Disney pop star— impossibly tiny with huge, liquid brown eyes and long honey colored hair pulled up high on her head in an *I Dream of Genie* ponytail.

I took her outstretched hand, and she gave me a firm, brief shake.

"Dr. Klein," she said, looking directly into my eyes. "I'm a psychiatry resident, and I'll be handling your case along with Blaire, who is a social work intern. She gestured to an even younger woman wearing a rockabilly-style dress that seemed overly cheerful for a psychiatric hospital. I shook her hand too but gazed past her, longingly, at the older doctors who were milling around the lobby, genially greeting their patients. I was skeptical. Were these women really going to help me? Once again, I had been left with no other choice.

"I'll be with you shortly," Dr. Klein said with a curt nod. "Enjoy your breakfast."

They filed in behind the rest of the team, chatting and laughing with their co-workers as they entered the large conference room, getting ready for another day at work.

———

At breakfast, I sat at a table with Sam and a few of the other young patients. I hadn't been the only one who was drawn to Sam's magnetic personality. In the twenty-four hours she had been in the hospital, Sam had quickly become one of the most sought-after companions on the ward. I couldn't help feeling like I had been accepted into the cool crowd by the most popular girl in school when, at every mealtime, Sam made sure everyone moved over so that I could sit next to her at the table.

When I was younger, in my teens and twenties, I gobbled up memoirs and movies that portrayed characters suffering from mental illness or addiction. They had the appeal of the slow drive past a car crash on the side of a highway. *Wow, how terrible! At least it's not me!*

Now, having suffered from severe mental illness myself, I'm more sensitive to the portrayal of my peers. It makes me wince when I think about all the times patients in a psychiatric hospital are characterized as a wacky band of misfits when, in reality, they are as ill as any other patient spending their days and nights living on any other hospital ward.

And yet. While the "wacky band of misfits" trope is damaging, there is no denying that the social stratification on a psych ward is intense—not surprising when the living space is small, the stakes are high, and the personalities are strong. At 11 East, the atmosphere was as gossipy, dramatic, and cliquish as a high school TV show. Alliances were formed, adversaries were made, and romances ran hot and heavy, even in spite of the no-touching rule.

Sam had caught the eye of the ward's Queen Bee, Maddy, who had been living on 11 East for three months after a suicide attempt that had left her missing a leg and permanently wheelchair bound. She was twenty-three years old.

Maddy's witchy good looks, gallows humor, and mercurial moods made her the charismatic leader of the young patients on the ward. She and Sam shared an ill-fated romance, arms around each other's shoulders on movie nights and kisses stolen during the brief moments when the guards weren't looking in the "chill out" room.

I knew I belonged more in the thirty-something clique, who spent their days playing Scrabble, coloring mandalas, and flirting with Bryan, the handsome, bearded forty-year-old who was suffering from a major depressive episode following a surprise lung cancer diagnosis. But I only felt like being around Sam, so I tagged along with the millennial crowd. They didn't seem to mind. I was really quiet, anyway. It was like I wasn't even there.

The young crowd were a boisterous bunch. They liked to brag. Who had the highest dose of antipsychotic medication? Who had gone the furthest off the rails during a manic episode? And they loved to boast about their suicide attempts. Whose was the most gruesome? With her brutal story of jumping off a ten-story building and tearing her leg on a fence, Maddy always won, silencing the crowd.

The only people at the hospital I told about my suicide attempt and DPDR were the doctors and Sam. As far as anyone else knew, I had postpartum depression. I was too ashamed to let anyone else know the truth.

Aside from Sam, I did enjoy talking to another member of the young clique, Thomas. He was gentle and silly and sweet. Although he was only twenty-four, he looked at least fifteen years older. He couldn't stop overdosing on heroin and was scared he was going to do it again the minute he was released from the hospital. Thomas had been on 11 East for a couple of weeks by the time I arrived—his discharge was scheduled shortly after I got there.

Thomas had a huge crush on Patrick and could get me laughing and opening up a little bit as he went on about Patrick's lanky physique and light blue eyes.

On that first Monday I was on the ward, Thomas and I sat next to each other in watercolor class. I was creating a terrible painting of a red barn set against a blue sky, and Thomas glanced over at my work and giggled. Then his face turned serious.

"You know," he said, "I think you're going to be fine. I think you're going to get better. About a week ago, there was a woman in here around your age. She had postpartum depression too. Really bad. She had a three-month-old daughter at home. And the craziest thing? She was a psychiatrist!" He shook his head. "She was really nice.

Stayed for about a week." Thomas nodded, reflecting, as he turned back to his painting.

Much later, when we reconnected, I found out that the woman Thomas was speaking about that afternoon had been my sweet friend from The Clinic: Alison.

———

After breakfast on Monday morning, I met with Dr. Klein. There were small glass-walled cubicles throughout the ward, and doctors used them to meet privately with their patients—although anyone on the ward could watch your meeting through the windows.

My anxiety directly correlated with my level of derealization, and my jagged nerves made me feel like I was having the session inside a swamp-like dream, the pale green walls of the cubicle breathing along with me each time I exhaled. I knew that my stay at New York East was the end of the line. If we couldn't solve what was wrong with me here, then what was next? I imagined spending a lifetime of being institutionalized by the state, receiving electroconvulsive therapy while I floated through life alone, glassy eyed in a hospital gown. I started crying before the session, even before we sat down.

Dr. Klein spoke in a clipped and direct manner. She was young, but I could tell she was both confident in her practice and smart. We talked about our main goals, which were to get me out of the hospital and able to function enough so that I could go home and be the mother and wife I had imagined I would be.

Blaire, the social work intern, sat beside Dr. Klein, taking page after page of notes on a yellow legal pad. I resented her presence, her small and hungry eyes taking in my pain, which I knew she would be relaying back to her grad school advisor. I sensed that she couldn't believe her luck at landing such a ripe case study. My pain turned into a final project she could present to her class at the end of the semester.

As I had promised myself, I was explicit in my concern about having DPDR and that I wanted to discuss treatment options for the disorder. But like all the other doctors I had seen, Dr. Klein was insistent that the DPDR was nothing more than a symptom of anxiety, and she suggested numerous times that I cope with the feelings of unreality by "splashing water on my face when I felt the derealization coming on."

I wanted to believe her, that it was just a symptom that could be washed away with a visit to the bathroom sink, but the churning in my gut told me that just like everyone else, she was wrong. If it was a symptom, it would come and go. But it didn't. It never left.

Dr. Klein was smart, but her diagnoses were off the mark. In our first session, she announced that I had bipolar disorder, which had developed during the peripartum period and had worsened postpartum. Then she told me that I would be starting a high dose of lithium accompanied by an even higher dose of Seroquel—200 milligrams higher than the 50 milligrams I was currently taking.

I accepted the diagnosis, once again relieved to have an illness with both a name and a drug to treat it, but I never knew how Dr. Klein arrived at the conclusion that I was bipolar. I was depressed, yes, but I never had any episodes of mania. And this was the first time she was meeting with me; could she tell right away? I felt wary too. I knew lithium was heavy, and I worried it would turn me more into a hollow-eyed zombie than I already felt I was.

Much later, when I combed through the notes of my stay at 11 East, the only reasoning I could find behind the bipolar diagnosis was that I was "labile," meaning I could pull it together for a few minutes to express myself clearly in therapy sessions and then would burst into tears. To Dr. Klein, this showed I was rapid-cycling through manic and depressive moods. To me, I was trying to communicate as well as possible, but would break down because of the raw pain inherent to the situation I had entered. And because of the unrelenting reminder of my separation from Patrick and Nora.

The diagnostic notes also frequently referred to a previous "struggle with substance abuse." I always answered yes when asked if I had used drugs in the past and yes if I drank alcohol. I told the truth. In my twenties I had gone pretty hard, but looking back now, I believe I was partying just as much as the rest of my peers. We had just settled in the city and were reveling in the self-destructive yet thrilling up-all-night lifestyle available to the young and beautiful and free.

Was this substance abuse? I didn't think so. But my answers must have been jarring enough to make the doctors correlate my long-ago drug experimentation and social drinking to a strong signal of bipolarity. Even so, in the diagnostic notes it is specified that this "substance abuse" had occurred in my early twenties.

I was thirty-nine years old when I stepped onto the ward at New York East. I hadn't "abused" a substance other than alcohol since I was twenty-four. And as far as alcohol was concerned, I hadn't had a drink since before I became pregnant with Nora.

When I asked Patrick if he remembered why the doctors thought I was bipolar, he sighed heavily. "I don't know, honey. It seemed like every day, you were diagnosed with something new. They were just throwing things at the wall to see what stuck."

Like Dr. Abrams's magical three-week prediction, Dr. Klein had a similar prognosis.

"Listen," she said. "Mental illnesses that happen within the context of pregnancy will go away. This will go away. You will get better. If I saw you on the street five years from now, I could 99 percent bet that you would be completely off lithium, and that you would be completely fine."

Dr. Klein's words were enough to get me on board without asking any more questions. I would begin taking lithium that day.

At the end of the session, Dr. Klein looked directly at me and asked, "Are you still having thoughts of suicide?"

And I answered honestly: "No, I'm really not. Not anymore. I just want to get better."

Dr. Klein nodded. "Do you have any questions for me?"

"Yeah," I said, a fresh round of tears flowing. "Can I see my baby?" My voice broke and I rested my head in the palm of my hand. The constant cycle of hope and defeat was making me so tired.

Chapter Seventeen

Patrick was allowed to bring Nora to the hospital on two conditions: that we stay secluded in one of the glass-walled therapy sessions and that she stay on the ward for only one hour.

That Monday afternoon, Nora and Patrick ended up staying with me from 11:00 a.m. to 3:00 p.m. Dr. Klein put us in one of the more private offices and walked by every so often with a small smile and a nod of her head, tacitly acknowledging that she cared enough to help us break the rules.

Admittance to the ward at New York East was a more civil experience. A security guard was located outside the locked door and discreetly examined packages before letting visitors in. Visitors would walk down a long hallway lined with offices before arriving in the main room at 11 East, helping respect the patients' privacy.

On the day of Nora's first visit, I waited at the end of the hallway, already soaked in tears. And when Patrick and Nora walked through the door, I ran to them, loudly weeping and throwing my arms around them, wailing, "My baby, my baby." A nurse overseeing the reunion remarked under his breath, "Jeez, I feel like I'm watching my Nonna at a funeral." It was a dramatic display, but it felt true. I was in mourning.

The four hours we spent in the cubicle together flashed by in a tearful blur. Patrick and I passed Nora back and forth, taking turns feeding her bottles of formula and changing her and bouncing her in our arms. She wore little red and blue striped pajamas that covered her feet and snapped up the front. She was only five weeks old, but she was already so strong, holding her head up on her own and taking in the scene with her big eyes: the office, the lights, our faces.

The threads in my mind were tangled up in tight knots that day. I wanted to come home, but I was scared to come home. I wanted to be a mom, but I was scared to be a mom. I wanted to get well, but I didn't think anyone, or anything, could help me feel better.

Questions twisted around and around: *How would Nora survive with a mentally ill mom? Patrick with a mentally ill wife? Would he leave me? How would I go back to work?* I imagined that we would end up living back with my parents, maybe set up our home in their basement while my mother took me to doctor's appointments and helped me care for Nora. Patrick would ride back and forth into the city for work each day, miserable and exhausted on the commuter train. That wouldn't be so terrible. Or would it?

I spent those precious hours our family was together running through catastrophic scenario after catastrophic scenario. Patrick would say something that made sense for a moment, that calmed me down, but I couldn't hold onto his words. They slipped through my fingers like water, and I retreated back inside my head.

———

The nights and the mornings on the ward were the hardest—waking up and knowing you had to make it through another day and then counting down the hours, the minutes, the seconds until you could take your paper cup of meds and escape into a black and dreamless sleep.

Sam would stay up with the young clique, playing cards or watching movies. She was having the time of her life and would frequently remark that "coming here was the best decision of her life" and that she was "learning so much from everyone." I would have felt jealous, but I liked her too much.

Each time I ran to be first in line to receive my meds at 9:00 p.m., Sam would whine, "Stay and hang out with us! You're such an old lady!" But I would shake my head. "I can't," I would say; "I'm too tired." Sam would flap her hand at me, shooing me away. "Ahh, get outta here ya old granny," she would say, smiling, and then turn around to join her friends.

In my before life, I would have loved to play cards and watch movies and gossip and laugh, but I couldn't be around groups of people. It made me feel too raw, like they could see directly inside of me, at how sick I really was. And everyone aside from Patrick and Nora still seemed unreal to me, the alien proxies of people I might have enjoyed connecting with. That was always the most frightening part.

Instead, I took my meds, selected a book from the large library shelf in the common room, and headed to my bed, giving a half wave and half smile to the group, their rowdy card game already underway. I put the book, unopened, on the night table and lay down on the small and sterile pillow. I watched the red lights blinking steadily out the window as they guided the ships down the river through the inky darkness.

———

Early Tuesday morning, I was jolted out of my heavy sleep before dawn. Two women I had never seen before came clattering into the dark room, rolling a cart and flipping on the overhead lights. No one ever knocked before they came in, even if we were showering or changing or asleep.

I was still trying to force open my heavy lids when one of the nurses was already tying my upper arm with a torniquet. She tapped the fat vein bulging in the crook of my elbow and stuck a needle in, sucking out vial after vial of blood.

"What's this for?" I asked, my voice a croaked whisper.

"Lithium levels," one of the nurses replied. "Can't let you out until we make sure we got the right level in your bloodstream. Need to be checking this every morning."

She peeled a Band-Aid and stuck it on the wound, and they clattered back out into the hallway, forgetting to turn off the bright light. Sam stirred, but she had slept through the brief commotion.

I couldn't fall back asleep, and I stared at the ceiling, waiting for the wake-up call. I didn't know what time it was. Our room had no clocks.

When the wake-up call boomed through the speaker behind my headboard, I shot out of bed, always the first in line for vitals checks so that I could immediately run to the phones. I was weepy even as I was dialing, the numbers on the phone blurry and slippery beneath my trembling fingers. By the time Patrick picked up on the other end, I was heaving jagged sobs.

Sam would pass by and wag a finger at me.

"No tears, boo," she would say, tilting her head toward the nurses' station. "They're never gonna let you out if they think you're still depressed. You've gotta stop crying so you can be home with that beautiful baby of yours."

I was unable to pull myself together, though. Stopping the tears that poured all the guilt and frustration and exhaustion and fear and longing out of me seemed like an impossible feat.

Sam, giving up on her verbal warnings, would start standing in front of me while I broke down into the phone, day after day, ostensibly blocking the nurses' view of me with her soft, wide hips.

———

Every morning, as the team entered the ward, I would try to catch Dr. Klein's eye, hoping for some news, any news, about my release or diagnosis or medication. Anything that could provide me with a quick fix of hope. Every morning, she would return my eye contact briefly and offer a curt nod. "I'll be with you shortly," she would say, and I would be left to the interminable stretch of breakfast and a morning activity.

After the painfully long hours of microwaved eggs and creative dance therapy, Dr. Klein would find me and we would go into the suffocating cubicle, Blaire trailing behind her in a 1950s swing dress, clutching her legal pad.

That Tuesday morning, Dr. Klein had news.

"So," she began, "you had an MRI on your first night here."

I recalled the fleeting relief of the cool, dark cave of the MRI machine. I nodded.

"Well, it looks like they may have found a lesion on your left temporal lobe. This is the part of your brain where anxiety is manifested. So we're going to take a closer look. You'll meet with a sonographer later today."

My mind immediately flashed to Susannah Cahalan's book *Brain on Fire: My Month of Madness*, where she experiences symptoms of psychosis that are eventually linked to a rare neurological disorder and learns that it was actually the disorder that had been masquerading as mental illness.

I had enjoyed the book long before I became ill and then frequently reread passages throughout my breakdown. Her early symptoms so closely mirrored mine: the alien doppelgängers of the people she loved, the too bright colors and harsh contrasts, the horror brought on by glaring lights.

I felt a thin trickle of relief run through me. This was it, I thought. It was so simple. They could just cut me open and take out the sick part. And I would wake up, head bandaged and black-eyed, but I would be back to myself.

Later, when I became a member of a Facebook support group for people with DPDR and other dissociative disorders, I learned that *Brain on Fire* was like the New Testament for my fellow sufferers. Many members of the group put their names on months' long waiting lists for a chance to meet with Cahalan's doctor. None of them ever had any luck. No part of their brain could ever be removed that would relieve their suffering, no exorcism that could draw the evil out.

In the afternoon, hours after the sonographer waved his wand through my sticky, gelled hair, Dr. Klein approached me with the results. I could instantly see in her face that the news wasn't what I was hoping to hear. And it wasn't. I had a benign cyst.

"Well," Dr. Klein said, "the good news is that you won't have to have brain surgery."

I nodded, touching the back of my head where my head was still matted with ultrasound gel, the tears beginning their flow once again.

———

My family returned from their trip on Wednesday night and planned to visit me on Thursday afternoon. Zach and Celine and their two young daughters, Zoe and Mila, would be joining them. And Patrick and Nora would be there too—it would be Zach and Celine's first time meeting their new niece.

I was hurt that they hadn't flown home as soon as they found out I was in the hospital. They had excuses: They couldn't miss the wedding, they couldn't change the flight, and—my mom's favorite painful refrain—that this was between me and Patrick. We were a unit now, and we needed to learn how to manage on our own.

Their excuses filled me with a resentment that lingers even now. But at the time, I buried my ill feelings toward them, locked them away for another time. I couldn't help it; when you're sick, you still just really want your mom.

———

My brother and sister-in-law aren't easy. They live lavishly: exotic vacations, expensive meals composed of culinary foams, weeknight snacks at home of oysters and ice-cold bottles of white wine. They are always wanting—more, more, more. And they question why you wouldn't want the same—or why you couldn't afford to want the same—tossing out careless judgments that can feel like a ball kicked square in the gut, knocking the wind out of you. If you weren't living your life their way, what was wrong with you?

Their flashiness and criticisms often enraged Patrick, pushing him into petulant silences during holiday dinners, his arms crossed,

151

eyes focused into the middle distance. For me, though, it's different. Although I am Zach's older sister by six years, I can't help but find myself wanting to please and impress him. He seemed to live his life with such confidence. I sought his approval like I was a small child who still believed that he could light up the sun. When I thanked him for coming to visit, he replied, "Of course. Where else would I be?" And I beamed.

My brother and his wife were two of the only people throughout my illness that could consistently comfort me, help me relax, make me believe for a few moments that this really might not last forever. That I might be okay. For all their criticisms in the past, this was the one time where they never judged, never made me feel like I was abnormal. They still saw the true "me" underneath my illness and never wavered in their belief that I would resurface again.

My family arrived on the ward that day like a caravan. Strollers piled with coats, babies strapped in carriers, paper bags overloaded with food for me and gifts for Nora.

Patrick, Nora, my brother, Celine, my two nieces, and my mom and dad filed down the hall, and patients looked up from CNN and Scrabble, their searching eyes wondering who on the ward was deserving of all this commotion. In the moment, I forgave them for the abandonment, the cruel remarks, the criticisms and judgments. We kissed one another's wet cheeks, and I let myself collapse into the relief of being loved.

Celine gripped my shoulders tightly and pressed her forehead into mine, our wet eyelashes nearly touching. "I think of you," she said. "Every. Single. Day. I think of you. You will get well. You will come back to yourself." I had heard this so many times now and only halfheartedly believed it. But coming from Celine, the promise sounded like it could almost be true.

Our family piled into one of the larger cubicles, pushing tables out of the way and arranging the plastic office chairs into a circle where we could face one another—our backs facing the window so no one could see me crying.

We spent the next hour passing around the girls, Nora at six weeks and Mila only one year old, reveling in their soft skin, their silky hair, the grips of their tiny fingers. Zoe, at four, chatted shyly in French, her huge eyes expressing what she couldn't communicate to us in English.

Against the rules, Zach had snuck a cell phone inside the girls' stroller and took pictures of our daughters. It was like a deranged family reunion. During the hour they were there, I kept repeating, "I feel almost normal," as though the repetition could convince my family and myself that it was true.

Before the hour was up, Celine squeezed in next to me on the plastic chair.

"Look," she said. "I know what I had after Zoe was different from how you are suffering now. But I want to tell you. You will have to do some work in order to get better. Medication will help, but it will not cure you. When I was suffering after Zoe, I could not leave my house. I was terrified. I did not want to be outside. But you have to, you see? So, every day, someone came over—a friend or my sister or my Mum. And every day we did something, something small. On the first day, Vanessa came. She took me to the supermarket. I cried and cried. Said I could not do it. But she made me stay, buy food for dinner. I cried the whole time. But I did it. Then, the next day, we went for a walk with Zoe in the stroller. The day after that, Flavie came. We went to Marjane. Again, I cried. It was awful. But I did it. Every day, just a little bit at a time. It took a long time, many weeks. But by spring I felt a little better. And by summer I was okay. And you will get better too. But you cannot give up. You will have to try. Okay? You promise me; you promise me right now that you will try."

————

The following day, Zach and Celine returned home. Soon after, my relationship with Zach and Celine drifted back into its old patterns, and all the distances between us grew once again.

Still, Celine's words and the fierce love behind them that day in the hospital stayed with me. I can hear them clearly in my mind, even all these years later. Finally, someone had given me advice that made sense.

————

On Friday morning, the ward hummed with nervous energy. Fridays were discharge plan day, where patients would meet with their team and create a plan for leaving the hospital and going home. Everyone knew that discharge plan days meant you would still have to suffer through a long weekend in the ward, but on Monday the electronic lock would be released, freedom beckoning from the other side of the heavy door.

Although I had spent most of my time on the ward sobbing—in meetings, in family visits, in tai chi class—I had assumed the ten-day limit that had been promised in the beginning of my stay was up and I would be heading out those doors on Monday with the rest of the emancipated patients.

I sat in my morning spot—the bench in front of the phone that was closest to the wall—so that when I made my calls, I could lean my head against the graffitied wall and cry into the chipped paint. This was what I was doing when Blaire, the social work intern, came to collect me. She wore a fitted leather skirt, which I found insulting.

A low-level panic set in when I noticed there was no Dr. Klein in sight. Instead, she was trailed by an even younger, mousy girl who introduced herself as another social work intern who would be shadowing Blaire for the day and not to mind her; she would just be along taking notes. Dr. Klein was missing, and my intern had an intern. I knew in that moment that whatever news I was about to hear, it wasn't going to be good. Monday, Sam would leave, a new influx of patients would arrive, and I would still be sitting in the same spot each morning, shaking under the fluorescent lights, counting the hours until the relief of the end of another day.

"How about we go meet in the Chill Out Room," Blaire offered.

I heaved myself up from the bench and followed behind her, the other intern scampering alongside me.

The Chill Out Room was a narrow space that was striped with long, ultramodern orange and lime green couches that undulated in waves. The lights were dimmer in here and there was a stereo; the intention was to make the Chill Out Room a soothing respite from the rest of the ward. I never went in, the potential for being too close to another patient in the narrow space filling me with terror.

That day, with Blaire and the intern, my dissociation deepened in time with my heightened anxiety and the couches rose and fell, their nauseous colors assaulting me like I was on an amusement park ride in a bad dream.

I started to cry. "Sorry," I apologized to the intern. "I cry all the time. I have an infant at home." I had developed a habit of apologizing to everyone before I would burst into tears.

The intern shrugged. "I see it all day," she said, like she was already a weary pro.

I knew I wasn't here to receive my discharge plan, but still, I tried. "So, they said I would be going home after ten days? So, I'm leaving on Monday?"

"Who said you're leaving on Monday?" Blaire asked, nodding slowly.

155

"My husband told me the doctor said I would be staying for ten days."

"Yeah," Blaire said slowly. "I don't believe that's correct." She was relishing this moment, probably her first big opportunity to deliver horrible news to a patient. She would probably be presenting the whole exchange, detail for detail, in her graduate seminar that evening.

"But I have a baby at home. I need to get home. I'm on lithium. I feel better. Much better."

"The team doesn't think you're ready yet." Blaire cocked her head to one side. "We believe your coping skills are still too poor."

"How am I supposed to be coping? I have a six-week-old daughter at home. I'm sick. No one has straight answers for me. What am I doing wrong here?" I asked. I didn't feel like being polite. I hated Blaire.

"Wel-l-l. You cry all the time. You haven't stopped crying since you've gotten here. You only interact with one other patient. And each time you receive news that you don't like, you go running to the phones to call your husband or your parents. Do you think that's coping?" She sat back and folded her arms. I was dissociating intensely, but I swore I saw the hint of a smug smile creeping across her face.

"You'll be here at least another week," she said, saccharine and sharp. "I'm sorry that's not the news you wanted to hear."

"Another week like Friday?" I asked.

"Well, yes; you'll be here at least until Friday. But you will most likely stay the weekend, since we don't typically discharge patients until Monday. Maybe Tuesday, depending on when an outpatient program can take you."

I calculated the days in my head, counting on my fingers as I pressed them one by one into my thighs. The following Sunday was Mother's Day.

"But that means I'm going to miss Mother's Day. I'm going to have to celebrate my first Mother's Day in the psych ward?"

"Well, Nora will be allowed to visit. But, yes. I'm sorry," she said in a singsong tone, cocking her head again. "You will be here for Mother's Day. Okay!" Blaire said brightly, clapping her palms on her thighs. "Sound good?"

I immediately forgot about my poor coping skills and ran out of the room, heaving sobs as I ran to the phone to call Patrick, then my parents, to tell him the news.

————

Later that afternoon, my parents visited. It was the first time the three of us had been alone together since Nora was born. I brought them to the larger cubicle from the day before. I had discovered a dimmer switch that could give my brain a brief respite from the constant assault of the fluorescent lights.

"Look at you!" my mom exclaimed, holding me at arm's length before we sat down. "You lost the baby weight already. Look, you barely even have a belly."

I had to give her a weak smile. This had always been our greeting: proudly displaying a weight loss or bemoaning a gain. Even trapped inside my awful illness, I couldn't help but feel a bolt of serotonin every time someone commented on my smallness, or as I easily slid into my size 4 jeans each morning after a shower.

Since I had been at New York East, my persona had vacillated between helpless infant and petulant teen. After the events of the morning, I was fully inhabiting the latter mode, slumped in my chair with my baggy sweatshirt flopping over my hands, too-long bangs beginning to obscure my eyes.

"I give up," I announced. "I can't do this anymore."

My dad started to contort his face into the familiar sneer and then stopped himself.

"What do you mean you give up?" he asked. "You're not planning to hurt yourself again, are you?" His voice was low and his teeth almost clenched. I knew he was struggling to control himself before he unleashed one of his fear-induced rages.

"No," I said. "I don't think so, anyway. But I don't know what to do." I began to break.

"Honey," my dad said, jaw tight, "you have a little girl. Your daughter. The daughter you and Patrick named. Her name is Nora. And Nora needs her mom. And that's your responsibility. To be her mom."

"This isn't right, though," I sobbed. "Maybe I'm depressed, but there's something else wrong. I've been on all these medications . . ." I trailed off.

When I was a teenager, it was the height of the New York club scene in the late 1990s. I took my fair share of hallucinogens during those years, tripping almost weekly on acid, mushrooms, Ecstasy, mescaline—whatever our friends could get our hands on to sneak into the Limelight every weekend. Even now, the best way I can explain what living inside a dissociative state feels like is to relate it to my experiences on drugs. Except, in my illness, there was never any joy or revelation or connection. And the trip never ended. It just went on indefinitely.

In the fleeting moments of connection I had experienced with my dad when I was a young adult, I learned that he, too, was not a stranger to hallucinatory drugs, having been a medical student in Upstate New York in the late 1960s.

Under the dim lights of the cubicle that afternoon, I took my shot at getting him to understand the full depth of the pain I was in.

"Dad," I said, taking a deep breath before rushing into my explanation. "You know how when you take acid or mushrooms or something, and you're tripping, but you can go to the store, you know, to buy a soda or something, and you're completely out of your mind but can pull it together enough to get your drink and pay the guy at the counter. And you seem normal enough to the guy. Like he'd never be able to tell how messed up you really are. And you feel like . . . you feel like you're getting away with something. Well, that's how I feel. I feel like that all the time. How am I supposed to be a mother if I feel like that all the time? How am I supposed to feel like this for my whole life?" My voice cracked.

"But it's not going to be your whole life. The doctors said—," my mom began.

I cut her off. "The doctors haven't been right about anything, yet have they?" I snapped.

"Dad. Please," I begged. "What do you think is wrong with me?"

My dad palmed his creased forehead. "I think you're right, sweetie," he said. "I think you have some kind of dissociative disorder. And, yes, you're right. It can't be treated by medication, not usually, not right away."

"So, no one can help me? Right? That's why no one's been able to help me."

We were silent.

Finally, my dad spoke. "No, sweetie," he said slowly. "No, there are doctors that specialize in dissociative disorders." He breathed hard through his nose. "We're going to get you some help, honey. Mommy and I are going to find you some help."

Throughout the next week, my parents bought every book they could find on dissociative disorders and DPDR. After seeing his own patients all day, my dad sat in his study and searched through medical journals late into the night. Any breaks he had during his workday, he would spend on the phone with the National Alliance on Mental Health, assembling lists of psychiatrists who might be able to help me.

My mother had always held the role of caretaker in our family, but during my illness she tended toward a more edgy distance.

Even despite our history, even despite the pain he had caused me earlier in my life, even as clumsy and awkward as he was in shouldering the caretaker role, when I think of the parent who reached out their hand in the darkness and guided me through that horrible time, I think of my dad.

As we hugged goodbye that afternoon, I remembered the date: May 5th. Cinco de Mayo. My dad's birthday.

"I almost forgot," I said, smiling shyly. "Happy birthday, Dad."

He said nothing in reply; he just bent down to kiss me, his full mustache prickling the top of my head.

———

Patrick came to visit me early that evening, alone. We were quiet, on the couch in the common room, half paying attention to the local news on the large-screen TV.

At some point, someone changed the channel to VH1. An old video took over the screen—the Bee Gees, singing "How Deep Is Your Love?" Our wedding song.

How many ways, I wondered, could the world conspire to make my heart break?

Chapter Eighteen

Over the weekend, the lithium kicked in, and it kicked in hard. I was no longer depressed or anxious—I was no longer anything. Even if I wanted to cry, I couldn't. My emotions had gone blank, and my hands never stopped shaking.

The inability to cry was a positive development in that it made it seem to the staff on the ward that I was getting better. But the lithium had another side effect—it made my dissociation worse. I was still viewing the world through the scratched and filthy film of the glass box I was locked inside, but now I was trapped in the box while wearing a straitjacket. There was no way I was getting out.

I eventually learned that lithium is one of the worst drugs that can be prescribed for someone who is suffering from a dissociative disorder. It can make the patient's feelings of derealization and depersonalization much, much worse.

And I was hungry. Lithium and Seroquel, especially in the high doses I was taking, can increase your appetite to unimaginable levels, your craving for carbohydrates skyrocketing like you had spent the day plowing a field rather than slumped on a couch watching the CNN ticker swim past on the bottom of a television screen.

My mom and Patrick split up the days so that someone would always be there to keep me company. My mother came in the morning, bringing a bag of food from the gourmet shop in her Westchester town—fruit salad, tarragon chicken sandwiches on baguettes, and buttercream-frosted cupcakes that she encouraged me to share with my fellow patients but, instead, I hid in my room, scraping off the icing with my teeth before bedtime. In the late afternoons, Patrick arrived with my favorite big salads or everything bagels the size of my head, soft and smeared with cream cheese. I ate it all, along with the microwaved lasagna I ordered for every lunch and dinner, smacking my lips like it had been prepared in the kitchen of a five-star restaurant.

My prideful days of wearing size 4 jeans ended quickly—the weekend the lithium took hold marked the beginning of my very rapid fifty-pound weight gain.

———

Now that I was no longer able to cry, I was free to commence the exhausting game once again: fooling the staff into thinking I was well enough to leave. I didn't know what I would do once I got home—how I would care for Nora, how I would be a partner for Patrick, how I would teach. But I knew that being in the hospital wasn't helping; it was just another stop on my free fall through a sneaky trapdoor. Even if I was going to get better like everyone was promising, I knew it wasn't going to happen at 11 East. It was time to go.

———

One of the odd characteristics of someone who has DPDR is that to the outside observer, that person can present like they are doing just fine: going to work, having a coffee, chatting with a friend, acting like they are normal while, in actuality, they are spending every waking moment trudging their way through the hazy sludge inside the delusory world in which they are locked away. They are bone tired from the daily masquerade, but they can still do it. They can convince everyone that they are just as normal as you are. Without the depression forcing me to show my hand, I started to be able to perform this trick too.

My therapy notes from my second week at the hospital are peppered with cheery comments on my mood and behavior: *Patient participated spontaneously during Creative Arts Therapy. During closing remarks in Dance Therapy, patient reported feeling "great." Patient's affect was bright. Patient engages well with peers.* In Coping Skills group, I promised the therapist that if I ever experienced suicidal ideation again, I would employ strategies such as *coloring* and *listening to music* to get back on track. The doctors and therapists patted themselves on the back for their contribution to my swift recovery. The only people who could tell I was still as sick as ever were my family. I never pretended with them. I was too exhausted.

———

On the Monday of the second week at 11 East, I met with Dr. Klein and Blaire. They both complimented me on my absence of sobs, my vacant acquiescence far more preferable. Lithium had wiped the depression out clean, like I had taken an antibiotic for an ear infection. Only the brutal dissociation remained.

In the meeting I was proactive. I relayed Celine's plan for getting well: employing an arsenal of family and friends to hold my hand while I tentatively shuffled forward on my way back into the world. The plan really did appeal to me. I would slowly reenter my life, my loved ones walking alongside me, as I dipped my toes into the water, not quite having to shoulder the full responsibility of recovery on my own.

Dr. Klein loved it. "Yes," she said loudly, bringing her hands together in a strong clap. "Now you're thinking," she said, like I had cracked the case.

———

After my session with Dr. Klein on Monday, plans for my discharge began to be set in motion. On Tuesday, my mother and Patrick were called in to a family meeting with Dr. Klein and Blaire. Dr. Greene, who was the head psychiatrist on the unit, made a rare appearance as well.

We went over my plan. I would still be on the ward for another week. My two days without tears had been a good start, but I would have to prove myself by successfully navigating the stations of the psychiatric hospital obstacle course: speaking up in group, joining in games of Scrabble, chatting with the other patients at breakfast, and keeping my affect as smooth and clear as the surface of a frozen lake.

The team loved the idea of my gradual reentrance into the world while holding onto the hands of an arsenal of family and friends to guide me through simple activities—taking Nora for a walk, a trip to the grocery store, picking up a coffee at the bagel shop. Patrick and my mother would be in charge of mobilizing assistance from our loved ones as soon as possible.

And I would be returning to The Clinic the following Wednesday, the day after I came home. Patients who have extended stays in psychiatric hospitals need to be released to outpatient care, and The Clinic had told Dr. Klein that they would "take me back," as though I was a teenager who had been allowed back in school after a short-term suspension. In a little over a week, I would return right where I had left off.

My dad still hadn't found a psychiatrist who specialized in DPDR and was currently taking patients, but he was working day and night, reaching out to any connection he had. Even despite my hopelessness, I still believed that he would find me the doctor who held the magic key to unlocking my misery and that I wouldn't have to be back at The Clinic for long.

For most of the family meeting, though, we talked about Patrick. In every therapy note from that year, each time Patrick's name is mentioned, he is referred to as a "very devoted and loving husband." And he was. He is. But I took it for granted, expected it. What else would he be?

Most couples who endure the kind of trauma that we had don't make it. Taking on the role of caretaker to a severely mentally ill wife is too much of a burden to bear, leaving the marriage irreparably fractured. I was lucky, but I was wrapped up so tightly inside my mind that there was no room to feel gratitude. The family meeting was the first time Patrick expressed his own needs. I had forgotten that he had any.

Patrick also liked the plan of calling on friends and family to help us. There was no way, he said, that he would be able to continue shouldering the full responsibility of caring for me on his own. He wanted to go back to work; he needed, deserved, some sort of structure in his life, some sort of space that he could carve out as his own.

And he needed a break from talking about my illness. The constant ruminations, catastrophizing, pleas for reassurance weren't helping him, and they weren't helping me. We needed to start breaking the cycles that had been leading us nowhere. And as uncomfortable as it was, or as unfair as it seemed, it was time for me to start taking on some responsibility for my recovery. My mother agreed, the doctors agreed, and I had no other choice but to agree too.

———

Tuesday was Sam's last day. On Mondays there's a "house meeting" where all the patients, doctors, and social workers gather in a large circle and the patients who are scheduled to depart the following day have the opportunity to give a farewell speech.

Sam spoke like she had just been awarded a Golden Globe, thanking the doctors and nurses and social workers by name and becoming tearful when she reflected on how far she had come, how much she had learned, the friends she had made. As she spoke, I noticed Maddy, Sam's love interest, looking down, trying not to get caught crying too. Over the weekend, I had seen them watching the visiting symphony, arms draped over each other's shoulders, visibly moved by the music, by their connection.

It was an ill-fated romance. To me, to Maddy, to the other patients on the ward, Sam's future was looking bright. But Maddy's future was an abyss. She had been on the ward for three months, and there was no news on if and when she would be getting out.

———

Sam left me a note on my night table. She wrote that she knew that it had been a short period of time, but she already loved me. That I would be the best mommy ever to Nora and the best wife to Patrick. That I would get well and get back to teaching very soon. She left me her phone number, her email address, her Facebook page.

I kept the note until the day I was discharged and then threw it in the garbage, along with the toiletry case, the slipper socks, the leggings and blue T-shirt I had worn nearly every day. I wanted none of it, no reminders. If I threw everything out, I could start anew.

Sam worked as a barista at a coffee shop less than half a mile away from our apartment in Astoria. Once I was better, much better, when Nora was almost two, Patrick, Nora and I went to the coffee shop to try to find her, to show her that we had made it. But the manager had never heard of a Sam. She must have left a long time ago.

Sometimes I go on Facebook and search for "Sam, Astoria," but of course it leads me nowhere. I tell Patrick from time to time that one of my greatest wishes is to get to see her again.

———

After Sam left, I forced myself to join the thirty-something clique. I played endless games of Scrabble, colored mandalas, spoke up in all the groups. My new roommate was a beautiful, skeletal girl who never spoke. She refused to join at mealtimes and would only eat Baked Lays, lying in her bed across the room from me in the dark.

The leader of the clique, Sarah, told me cheerfully that she was glad to finally get to know me. Before, she only knew me by the nickname given to me by the other thirty-something patients on the ward: "The Sad Mom."

By the end of the week, my dad found her—the doctor who specialized in DPDR. It was the same doctor I had found in my desperate online searches. The same doctor who had written the seminal book I had been afraid to read. The same doctor who was a fifteen-minute cab ride across town from Dr. Cook's office. Dr. Elizabeth Sarris. And I had an appointment with her on the last day of the month, May 31st.

On Mother's Day, my mom and dad came with Patrick and Nora. They brought me flowers and cards and a cake shaped like a bouquet. I remember very little about the day except stuffing down the pain with the cake—and then at the ice cream sundae station after my family left.

A patient who was on one-to-one, twenty-four-hour supervision and spent her days drifting through the halls in her dressing gown trailed by a nurse had her daughter visiting for the day too. She was doing her little girl's hair, combing through the soft, black curls and clipping on bright plastic bows.

Later, I approached her. "You have a little girl too?" I asked. She looked up, blinking, noticing me for the first time. She said nothing, giving me a sad smile before turning away.

———

Monday, I got to have my discharge plan appointment, to make my going away speech during the morning house meeting.

The discharge appointment was just Dr. Klein and I, back in the glass-walled cubicle where we had begun. The plan was to have me return to The Clinic the following morning. I would remain there until the 31st, when I would begin my treatment with Dr. Sarris. Patrick's parents and sister were on deck to help me navigate my way back into the world and to help me with Nora. And after that, time seemed wide open. I would have to learn to fill it with learning to live with my illness, learning to be a good mom, learning to take responsibility for my recovery and myself.

Patrick would oversee distributing my medication—it would be hidden from me. Dr. Klein had made it known several times that if I overdosed on lithium, I would be in for a lot more than just a long nap.

In our last meeting, Dr. Klein told me she was proud, and that she still thought this wouldn't last forever. It might not be a linear recovery, but it would eventually be a full recovery. And that I would be a great mom.

At the end of the meeting, she asked what I was excited about doing, aside from spending time with Patrick and Nora. I blushed a little and said that I had some shopping to do, and thought I might buy some clothing that fit, besides leggings and T-shirts.

"Where, do you shop?" she asked.

"Um," I said, "I like that store Madewell."

"Oooooh," she squealed, breaking character. "I love Madewell!" She clapped her hands, giddy.

"Listen," she said taking both my hands, "you did well. And I wish you and your family the best of luck."

We both stood up. As I turned to leave, Dr. Klein called me back. "And Barrie," she said, "one more thing. I know you're going to have a good support system helping you get back on your feet, but it's not going to be like that forever. You're not going to have to be carted around like some sort of mental patient for the rest of your life."

We exchanged small, closed-mouthed smiles and turned to leave the glass-walled cubicle for the last time.

What a strange thing, I thought, for a psychiatrist to say.

———

At the house meeting, I thanked Dr. Klein for her help in saving out little family. She flushed and gave a satisfied nod. I didn't cry because I couldn't, and also because I didn't really believe the words I was saying. Dr. Klein had been nice, but she hadn't really helped us very much at all.

———

Patrick signed me out of 11 East the following morning. He was tender, holding me, helping me fold clothes, kissing my eyelids, my forehead. He was scared for what was to come—we all were—but he was excited for me to sleep next to him again, to be in our home as a family.

———

We took a taxi home—they queued up in front of the hospital. It was a brilliant May morning, already warm enough for a sundress.

The trees already dripped heavily with flowers—weeping cherry trees, silky pink dogwood petals, lacy apple blossoms. Couples walked hand in hand, cyclists clogged the bike lanes. Daffodils and red tulips proudly sprouted up from the medians in the street, waving to their admirers as they swayed in the faint breeze. It was too much, the beauty beginning to warp and drip, the happy faces of the couples, of the cyclists and pedestrians, turning cruel. I wasn't ready.

"I'm just going to put my head down in your lap in the cab, okay?" I asked Patrick.

He nodded, smoothing the back of my hair, already warmed through by the sun.

—————

When we arrived at the apartment, Patrick paid the driver and we scooted out of the cab, hooking index fingers.

"Feel better, ma'am," the driver called out after us, and we headed up the front stairs and into our apartment.

Nora was sitting on my father-in-law's lap, and I shyly reached for her. I sat down beside him and cradled my daughter, stroking her cheek with my index finger, and for the first time that I had seen, she cracked open her gummy mouth in a wide smile.

The house didn't look as strange to me as I had expected, and I felt momentarily safe inside its walls. It would be the outside world that would play cruel tricks on me, tormenting me for a long time to come.

The date was May 16. I had been separated from my family for eighteen days, and I didn't have anything to show for it at all.

Chapter Nineteen

Years later, I summoned the courage to ask Patrick to fill in the lost hours from April 28, 2017. The day I tried to disappear.

"I need a drink," he said, and he brought out two glasses and a bottle of prosecco that had been rolling around the bottom of the fridge for months. It was the only alcohol we had in the house.

After the bubbles faded, we took a sip. Patrick made a face. "Gross," he said, and we tried to laugh a little before he told me his story.

At around 7:30 a.m., Patrick had come into the living room , where I lay on my back, covered with a thin blanket. I had been out for a few hours. He was holding Nora with one hand and reached down to shake my foot with the other. We were late. I was supposed to be up and dressed and ready to leave for The Clinic by 7:00.

I thought that I might have been unconscious, but I wasn't. This I had learned before, from Dr. Klein at the hospital. But Patrick could tell something was wrong. My speech was slurred, and my eyes were dilated, the green irises giving way to pure black. I struggled to keep them open, wanting to slip back into sleep.

Patrick wouldn't let me; he kept shaking, growing angry. What the hell was going on? He yanked my arm, pulling me up into sitting position. And I told him what I had done.

"I took the pills, Babe," I told him. It sounded like my mouth was full of spit and marbles. "I took them all. I'm so sorry," and then I fell back onto the pillow, passing out again.

Nora, her tiny antennae sensing danger, began to wail. Patrick pulled out his phone to call my parents—his first instinct that, as a psychiatrist, my dad would know how to handle the situation. But my dad couldn't summon any professional medical acumen in the moment. He could only be my father.

Both my parents shouted into the phone. Patrick heard words like "overdose" and "respiratory arrest" and "slowed heart rate." They screamed over one another until Patrick hung up on them, Nora shrieking in his arms. Then he dialed 911.

The EMTs and police arrived quickly. There were a lot of them, and they were all men. Some of the police milled around our house, picking up objects, walking through bedrooms. They had seen this all before: passed out mom, OD'd, no sense of responsibility, no regard for her family, no capacity to care about anyone but herself.

One of the officers pulled Patrick aside, wanted to talk man-to-man.

"Listen, buddy," the officer said. "This is the time. You get out of this relationship now. You don't want some drug addict as a mother to your kid."

"You don't understand," Patrick said, breaking down. "She's sick. She's really sick."

"You'll see," the officer said, wagging a finger at Patrick. "Mark my words; better get out before it's too late."

174

An EMT had pulled me up and onto the bench where we kept our shoes stored. He pointed to my sneakers. "Put these on," he said—and watched me struggle with the laces.

Regarding the scene, Patrick felt so helpless. He was so angry at the police, the EMT, my parents. Me. And so afraid.

An EMT and police officer hoisted me up and dragged me down the stairs, out the door, and loaded me into the ambulance.

Patrick stood on the sidewalk, barefoot, still holding Nora, who had grown calm.

"Where we taking her?" an EMT asked.

Patrick, remembering what Dr. Weissman had said, yelled out, "New York East! Right over the Queensboro."

The ambulance pulled away, no lights or sirens. Patrick and Nora were left standing on the sidewalk, alone together.

Patrick went inside and called his parents. They live about two and a half hours away and are terrified of driving in the city, but my father-in-law made it to Queens in less than two hours. Patrick left Nora with her Pop-Pop and headed to the hospital to try to find me.

It took hours. New York East is a monolith, and no one could help. Patrick felt like he was walking in circles for an interminable amount of time. Shifts changed; he never spoke to the same person. Everyone had a different answer.

In the late afternoon, Patrick learned I was in the psych ER. New York East had a guard and an impenetrable door too. No one would let him in. Doctors, nurses, and assistants came and went through the heavy door. No one answered his pleas for help.

Finally, Patrick stopped a young resident, finished with his shift and heading out of the psych ER for the evening. He placed a hand on the doctor's shoulder and spoke low and hard. "I need. To find. My wife."

The resident hesitated, and then motioned for Patrick to follow him. Patrick got patted down, phone taken away, all the routine humiliations one is subject to upon entering the realm of the severely mentally ill.

When he found me, I was slowly waking up, fluttering my eyes. He took my hand, and I smiled up at him, weakly.

"I'm so sorry," I said, my voice hoarse. "I'm so sorry."

———

It was hours before I was brought upstairs to 11 East. I was endlessly interviewed by doctors, residents, interns, scribbling notes on their pads—checking my pulse, my temperature, my blood pressure until the procedures began to blur together. I enacted my eerie tick of smiling when I got to the most painful parts of my story, flashing a shy grin when I recounted how I had tried to die earlier that day.

———

When Patrick left me for the night, settled in my room, it was late. I was finally lucid, and he felt a brief reassurance when I was able to kiss him goodbye and say goodnight before he returned home to our little girl.

———

Patrick's parents stayed with him and Nora for the eighteen days I was in the hospital, taking time off from work. They stayed even after my parents returned home from their vacation. My in-laws didn't mind, and I don't think Patrick would have wanted my parents there anyway.

They helped with night feedings, took Nora for walks, pointed out the annuals blooming in the backyard—the cotton candy peonies, the silky white tulips, the lilac bush. My mother-in-law sang nursery rhymes to Nora, gently touching her nose with a soft index finger as Nora looked up at her from where she lay atop my mother-in-law's thighs. In the weeks I was gone, Nora had begun to smile.

Patrick and his parents never talked about me in the time they stayed at our home. No updates, no reports, no plans. They just played with Nora or listened to baseball games on the AM radio my father-in-law had brought. Sometimes they ordered in a pizza from the parlor down the street and ate a pie for dinner. Patrick could just come home and pretend he was having a lazy, late-spring evening with his family. He deserved that peace.

———

The bottle of prosecco was gone. We barely remembered drinking it. Patrick put the empty glasses in the sink and came back to me, sitting at the dining room table. He pulled me up from my seat and, without saying anything, took my hand, both of us wiping our eyes a bit as we silently made our way to the bedroom.

Chapter Twenty

I teach middle-school English now, and we spend a lot of time on the hero's journey, walking alongside the characters in our books as they traverse an unfamiliar world, overcome seemingly insurmountable obstacles, and gain the courage and knowledge that allows them to return home—grown, changed, triumphant.

The classic conceptualization of the hero's journey is that it contains seventeen stages, but it can easily be broken down into three: the departure, the initiation, and the return. In the departure stage, the hero leaves the familiar world behind. Upon reaching the initiation stage, the hero must learn to successfully navigate the new, unfamiliar world. Finally, the hero has learned and grown enough to enter the return stage, the stage when they are able to return to the familiar world. When they can come home.

After the second hospitalization, I tried desperately to pretend to myself, my friends, my family that I had returned. But this was not the case. I had to stay in the initiation stage, learning to navigate the unfamiliar world I fell into for years until I was finally allowed to come home.

———

On my first day back at The Clinic, I dressed carefully and put on makeup. I tried to emulate Dr. Klein's *I Dream of Genie* ponytail and fastened my hair neatly atop the crown of my head, readying myself for the first of many false returns.

I also dressed Nora in a new outfit, a little navy blue onesie and rainbow-striped leggings, tiny socks designed to make it look like she was wearing Mary Janes. I snapped a photo, a routine I would continue each day for the next year, dressing her carefully and capturing the outfit and her smile. I needed to remember. I never wanted to lose any time again.

I packed Nora's backpack on my own, a new feat that I had previously been unable to manage, filling the bag with diapers, formula, wipes, changes of clothes, muslin burp cloths.

Everything I did that morning was careful and deliberate, as though by following this pristine ritual, I would be able to leave the previous months behind me and reemerge from the darkness as a radiant, perfect mother.

———

Nora and I would travel to The Clinic alone. Patrick would return to work. My mother would pick Nora and me up at the end of the day. We were play-acting at normalcy, hoping that might speed the recovery along.

In the car on the way to Manhattan, I would feel a brief relief as the car hurtled through the Midtown Tunnel—any moment of darkness, however fleeting, providing a respite from the harsh light of day.

———

The Clinic had changed in the weeks I was gone. The staff cooed over Nora and remarked on how well I looked, but other than that, no one paid much attention to us for the brief time we were back. There had been a huge influx of new patients—all white, all impeccably dressed. Some had personal drivers to bring them to and from their homes in upscale suburban towns in Westchester and New Jersey.

They seemed friendly with one another, talking about haircuts, clothes, their husbands, and other kids they had at home. One of the mothers was busy planning a birthday party for her older twins with a bounce castle, magicians, live music. The golden Gucci insignia gleamed on her slip-on loafers.

I know the other women at The Clinic were sick too. Some of them had just completed weeklong stays on wards for postpartum depression or anxiety. Some had severe attachment issues and were suffering from the inability to connect with their babies. I don't begrudge them or their swift recoveries. But I knew I was an outsider. I still hadn't found anyone else who had a dissociative disorder like me.

Mostly, the new mothers ignored me. I was very quiet, and I still had a strange affect. The lithium had wiped clean my depression and anxiety like my emotions had been sanitized with bleach, but I was still left with the worst symptom—the dissociation. The solid pane of glass remained unmovable, separating me from the other women. I was zipped as tightly as ever inside my plastic garment bag, unable to reach out, unable to connect. I spent group therapy sessions holding a large legal pad in front of me, creating a physical barrier between

181

myself and the rest of the room, occasionally jotting down notes so that I looked like I was keeping busy.

The Clinic was beginning to get a lot of publicity. It had opened only shortly before I had arrived in April but had quickly gained the attention of major news outlets, magazines, and morning TV shows with its pitch that it was the first of its kind, a luxe and soothing facility catering to new mothers who needed their help. Photographers came in often for stylized shoots of the staff, who had their hair blown out and their makeup perfected. And specialists began to arrive almost daily, giving PowerPoint presentations on sleep training and breastfeeding, empathetic smiles pasted on their faces as they pointed the remote clicker at the whiteboard. Even the creator of the SNOO came to present his $1,500 bassinet that promised to lull your infant to sleep almost instantly by simulating the sensations your baby experienced in the womb.

The staff tested it out on Nora while I was busy in a therapy session. I came back from the session and went to check on her in the nursery, and she was sound asleep, wrapped in the beige netting that's supposed to act as a swaddle. To me it looked like a straitjacket. I panicked and turned off the rocker, frantically unzipping her and picking her up, out of the bassinet.

After a few days back at The Clinic, a social worker cheerfully informed me that I would be graduating early the following week. Nearly a week before, I was scheduled to meet with Dr. Sarris. The team at The Clinic felt I was recovered enough to start handling the responsibilities of new motherhood on my own, with or without a severe dissociative disorder. Even at the time, I knew I was graduating not because I was better but because they had no idea how to treat me. It was time for The Clinic to wash their hands of me. I was probably bad for business.

———

As planned, Patrick and I assembled a team to help me begin to navigate through both motherhood and life. The reality of having a hand to hold as I tentatively learned how to walk through the world quickly became a sharp contrast to the fantasy I had developed while in the hospital. I lasted about a week into this new plan before I politely told everyone who was trying to help to please, go away.

The first week, Patrick's parents stayed with us, but for me their presence was unbearable, making me feel suffocated inside my home. I know their intentions were in earnest, but I could not help but feel as though every move I made was being judged under watchful hawk eyes.

Patrick's mom did everything I could have dreamed of to help me: She washed dishes, shopped for food, told me to rest while she took Nora for a walk, but I resented every act of kindness. I concocted fantasies that she was doing these small favors out of spite, that she was out to prove how inept I was as a mother. I felt like I could hear her thoughts: how shameful it was that her son had married a mental patient who couldn't even manage a trip to the grocery store. I was desperate to show that I was on the road to recovery, and each time she held Nora, I quickly grabbed the baby away, back into what I believed was the safety of my own arms.

"No worries," I would say. "I got it."

After the week they stayed with us, Patrick's parents returned to Pennsylvania, and we only saw them twice more before Christmastime. My sister-in-law Leigh is a single mother and was living in Patrick's parents' home at the time, and they were consumed with helping her raise her own toddler, our niece Ella. They were busy.

When we brought up having them visit, they demurred, claiming they were afraid of driving in the city—a statement I found odd considering they had traveled back and forth without complaint the whole time I was at 11 East. Mostly, I think they were just afraid of me.

On Memorial Day weekend, the weekend before I was to start my treatment with Dr. Sarris, my sister-in-law came to stay with us. Leigh had always been one of my closest friends and confidantes; she was less like Patrick and more like me: loud, silly, impulsive. I adored her. But that Memorial Day weekend, her presence in our home filled me with venom. I hated seeing her ease with Nora, how Nora clung to her, how she slept in Leigh's arms. I hated how thin and beautiful she looked, how healthy and comfortable she was in her body and mind.

Leigh took me on my first trip to the grocery store. A big event. The bright lights and colors, rows and rows of fruit and canned vegetables, and plastic-wrapped packages of raw meat lining the back shelves made me feel like I had entered an oozing, pulsating nightmare. I broke out into a sweat, my breathing labored and shallow.

Leigh walked in front of me, pushing Nora in her stroller. When she turned back for a moment, she saw my face and drew in a sharp breath.

"Are you okay?" she asked, low and urgent.

"I'm fine," I hissed back through clenched teeth. "Just keep walking."

After that weekend, Leigh didn't visit us again for a long time either.

———

The only outsider I could handle at that point was my mom. And she finally seemed ready to help. That late spring and early summer, my mom sat beside me on our couch several afternoons a week. She led me firmly yet gently through the small tasks we had come up with

184

during my discharge plan at the hospital: taking Nora out for short walks, buying a coffee at the bagel store. As the summer wore on, she took Nora and me out to quiet restaurants for lunch until I could sit through a meal without succumbing to my panic. She always sat with me until Patrick came home from work. Nora would often sleep on her, wrapping her arms around my mother's soft body as far as they could reach, like a little baboon.

Nora's connection to my mother didn't bother me, though; it made me feel proud. Even now, when I'm on the phone with my mom, Nora will grab it from my hand and go into her bedroom, closing the door and whispering toddler secrets through the receiver that are only for her and my mother to know.

My mother encouraged me, telling me often that she could tell Nora and I were deeply connected, that she could see we belonged to each other. But I always felt guilty. My derealization didn't allow me to feel as close to Nora as I longed to be. My mother later told me she could see the "real" me fighting, battling so hard with the part of me that was sick, trying to snuff it out so the true Barrie could reemerge.

A lot of mothers say that infancy is the most difficult time, that it's exhausting, repetitive, boring. But I think I would have loved it, had I not been ill. I often scroll through the photographs of the early months of Nora's life, wishing that, if only for one day, one moment, I could get that time back and feel her tiny body in my arms now that I am well.

I was just commencing my initiation stage, pulling back the curtain and stepping into the unfamiliar world I had to learn to navigate on my own. Still, I was desperate to rush forward. I fought with a ferocity I had never known, trying to bypass the battle I needed to conquer before I earned my homecoming.

I started taking Nora out for long walks, sometimes for hours, crisscrossing northwest Queens. Little tan lines appeared in the chubby fold between her calf and her ankle, the part of her body that stuck out from the linen blanket I draped over her stroller, protecting her from the sun.

Each time I left the house was a dare. Could I do it? Could I reenter the world? Could I see the landscape again through clear eyes? And each time I returned home, I received the same answer, loud and clear: No, I couldn't. But still, I woke up every morning and tried again and again and again.

My appointment with Dr. Sarris fell on a Wednesday. My graduation from the clinic had occurred nearly a week before, and Patrick's family had returned home over the weekend. I wasn't scheduled to meet with the doctor until later in the afternoon, and the plan was for my mom to pick us up in Queens at 2:00 and drive Nora and me into the city. She would watch the baby in the waiting room while I had my session.

For the first time, I had hours to fill, just Nora and me, alone. With the empty time ahead of me, I became restless. And so May 31, 2017, not only marked the date of my first meeting with Dr. Sarris but also ended up marking the day of my first independent outing into the world as a new mom, as the new me.

As I had taken to doing, I dressed both myself and Nora for the occasion—the outing and the doctor's appointment. I wore a long black T-shirt dress and black ankle boots, throwing a denim jacket on top. I was hoping to show Dr. Sarris that I was chic and pulled-together, but with my new extra twenty pounds, and limbs vibrating with a lithium tremor, I looked more a mess than ever.

Nora, on the other hand, was growing more adorable by the minute, with her perfectly round head and her easy smile. I had bought her a mint green linen jumpsuit printed with tiny cherries and felt a fleeting but deep sense of joy as I snapped the suit over her newly chubby body.

I took a picture of her lying on our bed, grinning widely, and texted it to Patrick. Then, impulsively, I decided a photo wasn't enough. I would show Patrick how sweet our little girl looked in person.

The museum where Patrick worked was about a half-hour walk from our home. The walk would take Nora and me more than forty blocks down a busy avenue, crossing beneath the shadows of overhead trains and navigating a dangerous intersection before arriving at our destination.

I didn't want to give myself time to think and hastily packed the diaper bag, strapping Nora in the stroller as we bumped down the front stoop stairs and out into the world. I didn't even tell Patrick we were coming. I knew it would make him afraid, and he would tell me stop what I was doing and turn back.

The journey, unsurprisingly, was terrifying. The volume of the world was turned up to the highest possible decibel. Colors, smells, lights, honking cars, screaming overhead trains, pedestrians I imagined were privately judging me—this overweight, crazy woman dressed in black pushing her infant through hectic intersections. But I pressed on, keeping my eyes focused on Nora's face as the rumbling of the stroller lulled her to sleep.

I arrived at the museum soaked through with sweat and trembling, but we were safe. I had successfully completed my maiden voyage.

Unexpectedly, Patrick wasn't angry or concerned. He was thrilled. He marched our beautiful daughter through the offices. I kept my head down as everyone congratulated and cooed, still too afraid to interact with strangers.

Patrick and my mother frequently texted back and forth throughout the day: *How's she doing? Better? Worse? Same?* I knew the pin code on Patrick's phone and would sometimes spy on their conversations. The day I took Nora to visit Patrick, I found a message on their text thread. It read: *She brought Nora to visit me today. She did it by herself. I'm so proud of her.*

———

The afternoon was less successful. My mother was already aggravated when she came to pick us up. It was hot, there was traffic, there were no parking spots in our neighborhood. We were late. She hadn't realized that my first appointment with Dr. Sarris was scheduled to be an hour and a half long, twice the length of a normal session because it was my first. "What in God's name am I supposed to do with a two-month-old in a waiting room for all that time?" she snapped.

We were stuck in motionless traffic on the way into Manhattan on the Triboro Bridge. Nora, who rarely ever cried, always made an exception for New York City traffic, which would enrage her to the point of shrieking sobs, red blotches breaking out all over her angry face. From where we were trapped between cars, engulfed in Nora's screams, I had a clear view of the Hell Gate Bridge, looming over the East River. Bad omens everywhere.

———

The office was located in a nondescript stretch of beige apartment buildings on Central Park West. We arrived a few minutes before the appointment, sweaty and harried, my mother lugging Nora in her car seat carrier. We had parked in a garage, and I was already deep into a state of dissociation from the few moments I had been trapped inside the hot, exhaust-filled cave.

The waiting room was small and smelled of plug-in air freshener, years-out-of-date magazines on the tables, the staticky fuzz of the noise machines overwhelming the too small room. I focused on Nora's little bare feet bouncing in the carrier as I tried to breathe myself back into my body.

Dr. Sarris emerged from her office. "Barrie?" she asked, nodding briefly at my mother.

Dr. Sarris was close to my mother's age, in her sixties; but with her long wavy hair and toned figure in a tight wrap dress and platform sandals, she looked about thirty years younger. Out of the corner of my eye, I saw my mom do a double take.

"We'll head over to the park," my mom said. "I'll be back in an hour and a half."

Dr. Sarris cocked her head in the direction of her office, and I followed her in.

When I go for my sessions with Dr. Sarris now, every six weeks or so, I feel luxurious. I read, uninterrupted, on the subway, a respite from my responsibilities as a teacher, a mother, a wife. I tell her stories about Nora, about work, about Patrick. We laugh. Now that I can see clearly, I realize that her office has been curated to create an atmosphere of peace. There are carefully arranged statues of Buddha and Ganesh; low-lit lamps and large, lovely collage art canvases; leather recliners to stretch out on. I curl up inside the respite of my forty-five minutes away from the world.

But that first day, and for a long time after, Dr. Sarris's office was a vortex pulling me further into the terrifying depths of derealization. Buddha's smile mocking, the collage art sick as a Weimar-era cartoon, the low light giving off the orange glow of the underworld in Dante's

Inferno. I sat ramrod straight in the recliner, my feet planted firmly on the floor.

"Okay," Dr. Sarris began. "I have your notes from the hospital and from The Clinic, but I'm going to ask you to tell your story again. From the beginning."

For the first time in weeks, I broke through the lithium chains and began to wail, eking out my story through choked sobs.

When I finished, Dr. Sarris appeared unmoved. "What's your level of derealization now?" she asked coolly. "On a level of 1 to 10."

"Like an 11!" I shrieked.

She let me take a few deep breaths as I tried to compose myself.

———

Once my sobs subsided into jagged breaths, Dr. Sarris continued.

"You have depersonalization derealization disorder," she said, her words confirming what I had suspected all along. My worst fears.

She explained that the DPDR had been brought on by several months of major depressive disorder that was left untreated and had become a more-severe agitated depression. That this was why the doctors at the hospital had diagnosed me with bipolar disorder, since symptoms of agitated depression can mirror those that occur during manic episodes or psychosis. And that, ultimately, the DPDR had likely been caused by my discontinuation of antidepressants prior to pregnancy, after having been on them for so many years.

———

"We will be able to treat the depression with medication," she went on. "However, the dissociation will most likely remain. It's unable to be directly treated with medication."

Although I knew this would be the diagnosis, had known it almost all along, her words still felt like a death sentence. A fresh round of sobs undulated through my body.

"Now," Dr. Sarris continued, "I can't tell you how long the dissociation will continue, and I cannot tell you if and when it will go away. Same as an oncologist when they diagnose a patient with cancer; they cannot predict remission or when it will occur, if it does. I do not have a crystal ball, so I encourage you to not continue asking me when you will get well. I do not know."

In that moment, I had the thought I later learned was shared by many fellow sufferers of DPDR: that cancer, or any potentially terminal illness, would be preferable to going through life like this.

"We will be taking you off lithium, which I don't believe is in any way helpful, and will put you back on Zoloft and a small dose of Klonopin. I will also be putting you on a medication called clomipramine, which should ease some of the obsessive thinking associated with DPDR. We'll see how you do. Any questions?" she asked.

I wanted to ask her if she thought I would get better and when that would be, but I bit my tongue, shaking my head. This woman was terrifying.

"What I can offer you is that, in my opinion, I do believe that, since this disorder occurred within the context of pregnancy, it will eventually go away, the further we get from the postpartum period. But it will take time. How long? I don't know, and I will not waste my time making predictions."

"So," I began shakily, "what do I do now?"

"You're going to live your life," she said.

"What do you mean?"

"You're going to be a wife, a mother, an adult, and you're going to live your life."

"How?"

"Each day, you're going to choose an activity to do with Nora that involves other new mothers. Find a group in your neighborhood and join. If there's no activity that day, you're going to see friends. You're going to live your life as though you're a new mother, just like any other new mother."

Dr. Sarris was prescribing exposure therapy, a therapy that involves the patient putting themselves in situations they would deem terrifying until the terror slowly diminishes and the situation just becomes a part of normal life again. It is painful and brutal, and it takes an exquisitely long amount of time to have any affect.

There would be no curative pill, no sessions where I leaned back in the recliner and recounted being teased in middle school, no rehashing my history with unavailable men. Just seemingly insurmountable work that I would have to perform, that might or might not even pay off in the end. I couldn't do it.

"I can't do this," I said.

"You can. You have to," Dr. Sarris replied.

"I'm not ready to put myself in these situations."

"Why?" Dr. Sarris asked. "A mommy group? A coffee date with a friend? What's the worst thing that can happen? You're not going to die, are you?" She glanced at her watch. "We have about fifteen minutes left. Anything else you'd like to discuss?"

"Are there any support groups for people with DPDR?" I asked.

"You know, a lot of patients ask me that; but no, not that I know of. You can check online, but I don't believe so."

We fell silent, staring at each other across the gulf between our recliners.

"So that's all you want to talk about?" she asked, raising an eyebrow. "Your diagnosis? You don't want to tell me about your career? Your marriage?"

I shook my head.

We sat in silence until she looked at her watch again. "Time's up."

I walked back into the waiting room where Nora was napping in her carrier, and my mom looked up at me expectantly.

"So?" my mom asked. "How was it?"

I shook my head, saying nothing.

———

I've never found another mother who had a diagnosis like mine. There was an abundance of support groups for mothers who suffered from postpartum depression, postpartum anxiety, postpartum psychosis, postpartum bipolarity.

I was envious of these communities where diagnoses could be explained in short, declarative sentences, so simple they could be printed in a basal reader: *I am depressed. I am anxious. I am manic. I am psychotic.*

DPDR had to be described in dreamy conjunctions, struggling to link a creepy fantasy realm to a neurotypical reality: *I feel as if . . . , I feel as though . . .*

The only books about my disorder had nightmarish covers; the online portals had eerie sounding web addresses like *dreamchild.net*.

I always told people that I had suffered from postpartum depression. If I got close to someone, I would tell them that I had postpartum psychosis. It was just easier that way.

Later, when I began to manically consume mental health memoirs, I read Esmé Weijun Wang's brilliant essay collection, *The Collected Schizophrenias*. In the book she writes: "Some people dislike diagnoses, disagreeably calling them, boxes and labels, but I've always found comfort in preexisting conditions; I like to know that I'm not pioneering an inexplicable experience."

I would have given anything for a label, a box, a checkmark on a chart. I would have given anything not to be a pioneer in this surreal nightmare.

Recovery is long, winding, painful, boring. Patrick would later call my recovery period a "slog." I couldn't have come up with a better word to describe the next eighteen months.

After a few months of growing accustomed to my assigned exposure therapy tasks, I began to view myself as someone who was learning to live with a chronic illness or impairment. I was deaf, I was blind, I had MS, I had early-onset Alzheimer's. Except it seemed like everyone else had a community to lean on. I had to do this alone.

———

I found a local parent group on Facebook whose members seemed pleasant enough in the supportive messages they left for one another in the comment threads. There were meetups almost daily—in parks, in coffee shops, in yoga studios—and once a week they got together at one mother's home for tea and conversation and a playgroup for the babies.

The first meetup I chose to attend was in the backyard of a local coffee house. I circled the block three times before deciding I couldn't do it. I couldn't go in. I took Nora to a playground instead, where she was too young to do anything except lie down in her stroller. Being outside and around other mothers had to count for something, didn't it? Even though I didn't interact with anyone.

Patrick began helping me choose an activity to do with Nora the night before, to give me a gentle push as well as to hold me accountable. The first activity I attended was the tea and playgroup for new mothers. I was so scared they would somehow be able to tell that I was sick, that I had been hospitalized, that I had wanted to die. I was scared they would judge me for not breastfeeding, for taking medication, for not being the natural earth mother I was supposed to be. I imagined they would be sitting in a circle, already slim in their yoga clothes, silently judging me with their eyes as they held their babies to full breasts.

When I entered the apartment where the playgroup was being held, I was dissociating so hard that the living room seemed to tilt and spin as though I was on a carnival ride. But I was welcomed. I sat down in the circle with the other moms. I could sense that most of them were anxious and vulnerable too. And I wasn't the only mom in the group who bottle-fed.

The mothers were friendly but not overbearing. I chose a new meetup every night with Patrick and attended every morning. I came home every afternoon, exhausted, lying in the same position on the couch as Nora slept on my chest, steadying me with her weight. I watched endless episodes of TV series, only half paying attention.

Nora and I took cars into the city, and we sat in Dr. Sarris's office twice a week, where I had therapy while holding her in my arms or jiggling her in her car seat. I tried to make the world come back into focus. I returned home defeated. We waited for Patrick to come home from work. And repeat.

Chapter Twenty-One

In the late spring of 2017, I didn't look like I had just been released from an eighteen-day stay in a psychiatric ward, that after mommy-and-me playgroup, I would be heading into Manhattan for intensive sessions with my psychiatrist. I looked like I saw the world through the same clear-eyed lens as everyone else.

As spring turned to summer and the months rolled on, I became excellent at hiding my mental illness, my deftness at keeping up appearances and mirroring social cues serving me well.

Like any other New York City mom, I wore my faded Levi's, my high-heeled clogs, a messy bun perched on top of my head. I was a little heavy, but I could use that as a way to connect and commiserate. No one needed to know that my heaviness was actually from the prescribed drug cocktail I had titrated on and off of for months. I was like a cool mom automaton. My voice must have spoken all the right words, but to me it sounded tinny because, inside, I still felt hollow.

Even if anyone did perceive that something about me might be a little off, it was easy to be distracted by the baby grinning out into the world from where she was snugly strapped to my chest in her carrier.

Nora loved people. She would turn her head to one side, raise her eyebrows, and offer admirers a sly smile, like she was in on the joke. She laughed if you sniffed her feet and had thigh rolls that begged to be bitten. On warm days she wore soft, linen jumpsuits printed with fruit or flowers or polka dots. When closed, her eyes had faint purple webbing on the lids. When open, she had Patrick's crystalline eyes. At two and a half months, Nora was simple perfection. She still is. I couldn't make it down a single block without someone stopping me to remark on her beauty, her smile, her eyes.

My daily outings with Nora became bolder. We went into stores and I tried on clothes in the dressing rooms. A good friend brought us to Jones Beach for the day. I took Nora on Metro-North by myself to visit my parents. All the friends we had avoided seeing started coming over, bringing the gifts they had saved for months. *I had severe postpartum depression*, I would tell them, *but I'm fine now.* We kept walking. I pushed her stroller forward on the scorched sidewalks, waiting for a change.

———

In my twice-weekly sessions with Dr. Sarris, I was usually frustrated and sullen, annoyed at the $600-a-week cost and annoyed with her therapy style, which was of the silent séance variety.

Dr. Sarris's actionable steps have always been sharply insightful. Although it may have been unbearably slow, each step she made me take did end up moving me forward.

Her analyses, however, were awkward. Often, dissociative disorders stem from a severe trauma experienced in the sufferer's life, and so the patient dissociates from the world, ostensibly protecting them from further harm.

Dr. Sarris wanted to dig into my history with my parents, the verbal and emotional abuse I had endured from my dad, the unwillingness of my mother to protect me from it. It was awful growing up in that environment—fearful, unprotected, unsupported, believing I was unloved. And my father's treatment of me did, I believe, lead to my low self-worth in my relationships with my friends, with men, with myself. It led to my anxiety. It led to my depression.

But my father and I had reached a sort of denouement nearly twenty years before. Our relationship isn't perfect, but I do believe that I forgave him, that I processed what he put me through, that I stopped blaming him. Mostly for my own sake.

Dr. Sarris kept returning to my father's emotional abuse, insisting that we claim the experience as traumatic, but I couldn't find it within myself to believe that it was enough to make me completely dissociate from reality nearly twenty-five years after the fact.

———

I often told Dr. Sarris that before I had gotten sick, I was happy. I was confident. I had come a long way from my painful and damaging childhood. I told her that I wished she could have known me during those long years of being joyful and self-assured. I think she believed I was crafting an imaginary version of my prior self. There was no way this sullen child who sat before her could have been the woman I was describing.

Recently, when I asked her about our first sessions, Dr. Sarris said she was surprised at how acute I still was, how raw and needy. "You were like an infant," she told me. "You just wanted someone to take care of you, to make it better. I wouldn't let you. I made you be the adult, the mother. There was only room for one infant, and that was Nora."

———

I don't know why I hadn't thought of it before, but I began to flash back to the other two times I had tried to wean myself off anti-depressants—and the resulting aftermath.

When I had been prescribed antidepressants, I was twenty-two, a graduate student living on my own for the first time in the city, struggling with panic attacks and seemingly interminable periods when I could barely pull myself out of bed. And the medication was effective. Antidepressants eased my struggles with depression and anxiety, allowing me to move more freely through the world. I stayed on the medication. It helped.

I saw a psychiatrist regularly in the beginning, but I soon stopped. At more than $100 a week, I couldn't afford it. Not when I was a twenty-two-year-old student. I found that the medication was easy enough to refill anyway—any general practitioner will prescribe you six months' worth for a simple co-pay of $25. And you didn't have to waste your time sitting through therapy sessions, rehashing the same story.

But still. Even though antidepressants were helpful—even though I probably needed them to treat my depression, my anxiety, to keep me healthy and sane—I couldn't quite shake the feeling there was some sort of unspoken stigma attached to taking medication for an illness that was invisible. To me, taking an antidepressant quietly implied that I was mentally ill. And no matter how much anxiety and depression became normalized, I still resisted attaching that label to myself.

So I tried to go off them. Twice. Twice when I was feeling happy, ready to be "normal," not realizing it was the medication that was helping me feel this way.

I titrated down little by little, week by week, until I was cutting the pills into slivers. I didn't do it without the guidance of a doctor—I asked whatever general practitioner I was seeing at the time, whoever was refilling my script twice a year, and of course they said "sure." What did they care? They didn't know anything about me.

Both times, by the end of my titration, by the time I ingested my last bitter slice of pill, I was hit with a depression so severe, I can only liken it to dying by slowly being crushed to death by a barbell dropped on your chest, another weight added day after day.

Both times, I missed days of work. Both times, a friend had to come to my rescue, scooping me off my couch where I lay, un showered and curled into myself as I silently recounted everything I had ever done wrong. I was taken back to whatever general practitioner I had been seeing, and the doctor put back on medication again just as nonchalantly as I had been taken off. And a week later, I was better. I had caught it in time.

When I decided to take myself off antidepressants for the third time, that spring before I got pregnant with Nora, I did it on my own. This time, I was really fine, I reasoned. I had a great job, a great apartment, great friends. I jogged, for God's sake. And, most importantly, I was married. The crowning achievement in what I imagined adult stability to be.

This time, after the last sliver was ingested, the depression took a little bit longer to take hold—a few months of barely perceptible shifts, thinking I had made it—until I was flung backward onto the couch, the weights crushing my chest, holding me down with such force, I had lost the chance to set myself free.

The message filtering through the ether seemed clear: If you take medication, you're going to hurt your baby. You're being selfish. You're a Bad Mom. When we had turned to my ob-gyn for help and he referred us to the reproductive psychiatrist, who only offered natural remedies instead of prescription drugs, the message was compounded. It was slammed into our heads.

No doctors nonchalantly allow a diabetic patient to go off insulin on their own. Same with medications for heart disease, cancers, stroke victims, even high blood pressure. Depression is just as chronic and just as life threatening, but is rarely treated as such.

Sometime during that first summer, I told Dr. Sarris that I thought my acute condition hadn't been caused by an unhappy childhood but rather had been caused by leaving a severe, chronic illness untreated for so long that it had become too late. She didn't disagree.

———

I tried to learn more about my condition. I bought the books with the trippy, sinister covers; I lurked in the AOL-style chatrooms; I clicked around dreamchild.net. But there was so little concrete information on DPDR, and the information that did exist was weird.

There are a lot of notions and theories floating around that DPDR can be reframed as a spiritual awakening or a road to enlightenment. These theories are not just drummed up by patients who are trying to take some kind of ownership of their condition but also by doctors, therapists, and medical professionals. As though having DPDR was just as lovely as experiencing a revelation about the universe while you come down from your acid trip, watching the sun rise over the yucca plants at Joshua Tree.

I didn't buy it. Thankfully, neither did Dr. Sarris. In researching my disorder early on that summer, I came across a 2014 article in *The Atlantic* on DPDR. In the article, Dr. Sarris is quoted: "People suffering from depersonalization disorder don't appear at a doctor's

Barrie Miskin

or a psychiatrist's office to explore mysticism, philosophy, or the deep blue sea. They make the appointment because they are in pain."

It was that quote that let me know I could trust Dr. Sarris. That she understood. That she wanted to help. It kept me coming back to her week after week, seeking her guidance. I know those words by heart.

———

As Dr. Sarris had predicted, by late summer the depression began to lift. With the loosening of the depression, the dissociation remitted slightly as well. I was no longer trapped in a straitjacket, imprisoned inside a tiny, filthy glass box. Instead, I felt as though I now viewed the world from inside a small, hot car with dirty windows that never rolled down and doors that never unlocked. It was better than the straitjacket and tiny glass box, but it still was no way to live. Apart from a few merciful moments of respite, I remained inside that locked car for nearly a year.

Even with the torturous discomfort of my disorder, though, I was able to enjoy my time with Nora. Since birth, Nora has steadily maintained the same personality: smart, funny, and loving. I still call her my "easy baby." She's good company.

Since she was an infant, she's found ways to let me know she belonged to me. She smiled and laughed when I entered a room; she napped for hours with her head on my chest. It was me she reached for, each time.

Our favorite outing together was going to the library for sing-along and story time. Since I was small, the library has always been a haven: the hush; the sweet, musky book smell; the expectation that you would be left alone for hours as you disappeared inside its homey embrace.

The library was less than a block away from our house, and the librarian who led the story time was gentle and kind. She would tuck her long skirt beneath her before she sat down in her chair, taking a small breath before she opened a book and began to read in her soft, patient voice.

The babies in the group mostly wriggled and cried, but Nora would sit in my lap, her attention rapt, staring at the librarian until the story was done.

At the end of story time, the librarian would sing songs, the adults singing along as they bounced the babies in time to the beat of the rhyming words. There was one song Nora loved, something about zooming to the moon. At the end of the song, there was a countdown, and once we got to "blast-off," the adults lifted the babies in the air like rocket ships. Each time, Nora shrieked with delight. I can still feel her compact little body in her denim overalls, the buckles and snaps underneath my palms as she screamed and laughed when I raised her into the air. It was in these times that I could access brief flashes of joy. It was buried, it was just out of reach, but it was still there. It was still within me.

Mornings were always hardest. It seems to be a common sentiment among people who suffer from mental illness that the pain is most acute at the start of the day. Hypothetically, this is caused by the body's hormonal shifts and circadian rhythm after a night of rest. More likely, though, is that morning serves as the brutal reminder that there are eighteen hours ahead to battle through.

But in the evenings, Patrick would come home and a peace would infiltrate our house as the light outside faded. The three of us would pile into our bed. Sometimes, Nora would doze and we would just lie there without speaking, counting the little wrinkles on the back of her neck as we breathed in the relief of making it through another day.

———

Sometime in early August, I received an email from my boss, Richard. Delicate and tactful as always, Richard asked how my summer had been and if I had secured childcare for Nora for the fall. I had already signed a contract before my maternity leave, stating my intent to return for another school year, but other than sending Richard a photo of Nora right after she was born, I hadn't been in touch with him at all, which was unusual for me. I knew the subtext of his email. He was asking if I would be well enough to return to work.

The question that Richard was asking was the question that had been looming over our family for months. In the back of my mind, I was still faintly holding on to the idea that we could move in with my parents, forgoing rent payment while my mother helped me care for Nora and Patrick commuted into the city each day on Metro-North.

Dr. Sarris and I had discussed my return to teaching several times. She pushed me toward going back. I resisted. How would I be able to teach a class of thirty six-year-olds when I felt so untethered to reality? By the time Richard's email arrived in the late days of summer, Dr. Sarris and I still hadn't reached a final conclusion.

I showed Dr. Sarris Richard's email at our next session. She put on her reading glasses, balanced at the tip of her nose, and briefly scanned the message. Then she wordlessly handed back my phone.

"You'll write him back today," she said. "And you'll let him know that you're prepared to return."

I closed my eyes and nodded. I was afraid, but I also felt a trickle of relief seeping in. Did going back to work mean that I was getting better? That I was returning to normal?

I was going to have to continue living my life *as if*. As if I wasn't suffering. As if I wasn't struggling. As if I wasn't mentally ill. I had reached the concrete basement floor on my descent through hell. There were no more trapdoors for me to fall through. I had two choices: I could either learn to live with a mental illness, or I could die. And I didn't want to die anymore. I wanted to stay here with Patrick and Nora.

I wrote Richard back the following day. *Yup! All set! Looking forward to seeing you soon.*

————

Richard was the kind of person to show he cared about you by performing subtle acts of kindness and never making a big deal about it, never asking for anything in return. I know he had heard through the grapevine that I was still not back to myself—one of my close friends at work is on the administrative team, and she discreetly warned him not to expect the Barrie he previously knew to be returning to work. She told him I was more quiet, more withdrawn, less confident—a contrast to the bright and self-assured woman he had worked with for the past six years. *Understood,* Richard told her. That was always his response: *Understood.*

Richard set up for my return to be as low-stress and comfortable as possible. He made sure supplies had been ordered for me and were already stored in boxes outside my classroom door. He also arranged for days where Patrick and Nora could come into school with me, slowly helping me reacclimate to being in the building, slowly setting up my classroom again to make it feel like my own.

Patrick hung up posters for me in places I couldn't reach and tightened the legs on the small tables my first graders would be gathered around in a few weeks. Nora rolled around happily on the huge, colorful rug where thirty bodies would soon be sitting crisscross applesauce, staring up at me with huge eyes, waiting for me to teach them how to read or add or discover their place in the world.

It made me nervous being there, but there was that small part of me, the same part that could access the faint hum of joy when I brought Nora to story time at the library, that could sense a vague hint of excitement. I had always loved my job and felt safe inside its measured routines. It was my second home.

The most significant kindness that Richard did for me, though, was giving me Elva, my associate. He let me know that she would work alongside me for the next two years.

Elva was my intern during my first year teaching at my school, and I had fallen in love with her right away. She was only twenty-four at the time and had just gotten married to her childhood sweetheart, Rob. They had been together since they were eleven.

Born and raised in Maspeth, Elva was a Queens girl through and through, with the loud, husky accent, long nails, and sharp tongue to prove it. If Elva loved you, you belonged to her for life. But if she didn't, you had better step out of her way. I was one of the lucky ones.

Elva and I had also worked together during the best year of both of our lives—the year before I got pregnant with Nora.

That year, Elva became pregnant with her son after a long fertility battle; at the same time, Patrick and I got engaged and then married soon after. We were both floating, giddy with excitement—and completely unprofessional. We spent the days laughing, gossiping, and planning for the chapters in our new lives. We didn't spend very much time teaching, though—or paying very much attention to the children.

But Richard knew that Elva was my family, that she would keep me feeling supported and safe upon my return, so he brought us back together. We knew this was a huge favor, but he did it without saying a word.

Aside from my family, Elva was really the only person who knew the extent of what I had gone through and how sick I truly still was. Every day, she showed up to work and sat across from me at our makeshift desk, holding my gaze and subtly nudging me to not give up, to never give up. To keep on going.

And she could make me laugh. Elva was the queen of malaprops. Example: If we were having a rough day and she felt like the stars were not aligned in our favor, she would claim that "Mars must be in retrospect." I would crack up, and each time I laughed, she would look at me proudly, across our little desk. "Ah, there she is," she would say, opening her arms wide. "She's back!" It made me feel better.

Elva didn't really think I had come back. Not yet. But she never gave up on me. She held me steady for the next two years. She made sure I stayed connected to the world.

My first year back in the classroom wasn't my strongest year teaching, but it wasn't my worst. The kids made it easy. They were charming and bright and so kind to one another that it was almost peculiar. And the administration left us alone that year, forgoing regularly scheduled observations until I was able to relocate my sense of equilibrium at work.

Elva kept me organized, reminding me of when I had to call a parent or turn in a report or attend a meeting. She would cover for me when my dissociation consumed me so much that I was unable to function.

Once, a student fell on the playground, splitting his lip so severely that he had to be taken to the Emergency Room in an ambulance. At the words "emergency room," I began dissociating to the point where I felt like I had completely floated out of my body, leaving only a husk behind. Elva told me to go home and lie down. She took care of the kids for the rest of the day and never mentioned the incident again.

I managed, but I came home exhausted. I rarely cried anymore, but I remember coming home one day in late September and breaking down. I sat slumped on our living room rug with my knees pulled up and my palms covering my face. "I'm just so uncomfortable," I said to Patrick in between sobs. "It's just so uncomfortable trying to live like this every day." Patrick put Nora on my lap and reached his arm around my shoulders. "We're here for you, Mommy," he said. "We're always here."

———

With all the time he had missed in the past year, Patrick had to reestablish himself at his job, and he became obsessive about regaining his footing at work. Since the busiest days at the museum were Saturdays and Sundays, Patrick was often gone all weekend, leaving me to take care of Nora on my own after teaching all week. My parents and my youngest brother, Alex, usually came in to spend time with us in the morning, having brunch or taking a walk to the local park, but they couldn't stay with me until the later evening hours when Patrick finally arrived back at the apartment.

During the week, Patrick worked late too. There was always an event or a deadline or a crisis. I would finish work and walk the two miles from my school to Nora's day care, pack her into the stroller, and roll her home. Day after day.

As evening came, Nora would sit in her bouncy chair, watching me chop ingredients for the dinner I would have on the table in time for Patrick's return. Then bath time, three books, bed. Day after day.

On the weekends, when Nora napped, I lay down next to her and fell into a sleep so heavy it was like I was being pulled downward through quicksand.

———

During that first fall and winter, it was like our family was being held in a liquid suspension. We remained quiet and still, petrified of sinking to the bottom.

I became obsessed with proving to the world that not only had I fully returned to myself, but that I was the perfect mom. I spent any free hours I had scrolling through the social media pages of mothers I wished I could be and then tried to reenact the idyllic scenarios they posted to their Instagram stories.

Here was Nora in a gingham jumpsuit at the farm. Here she was in overalls at the pumpkin patch. Here I am wearing cat ears, holding Nora dressed up as a golden retriever. I decorated the house for Christmas on November 9th. We had a photographer take our picture for family holiday cards. We sent them to everyone we knew. Even to my ob-gyn. Even to The Clinic. *See?* I pleaded. *See how wonderfully everything turned out?*

Patrick and I never fought during those months. I never complained. I never cried. We held our breath. I plummeted downward through dreamless sleeps.

———

One of the few respites I had that fall was Katie. Nora was in day care five days a week, a place so nurturing and magical, I still have a hard time believing it exists. Each day was a celebration: There was Elvis Day, 1920s Day, Red Carpet Day. And each day, parents were sent pictures of their babies wearing sunglasses or long beads or with their collars popped up like The King.

In the photos of Nora's little cohort, Patrick and I noticed that there was another baby in the class who looked uncannily like our daughter. Nora and the mystery look-alike were often posed next to each other, two gummy-smiled, blue-eyed towheads enjoying baby yoga, or baby Zumba, or baby karate class, side by side.

The teachers got them confused constantly. Almost every day, Nora was sent home with a coat, a lunchbox, or a bottle labeled "Tommy." After this had been happening for a few weeks, I reached out to Tommy's mom to apologize that we had unwittingly begun to hoard his tiny possessions.

Katie was as Midwest-nice as they come, responding to me right away with a friendliness that almost caught me off guard. She had tons of questions for me: Where was I from? What did I do? Oh, she loves teachers! How were we liking the day care? We loved it? Oh, wonderful! She loved it too. By the end of our chat, Katie had already invited me to get together that weekend at a new baby gym that had opened in our neighborhood. I was nervous to meet someone new, but the idea of breaking up the interminable stretch of the weekend alone won out. That Saturday, Nora would have her very first playdate.

Katie matched her sunny baby perfectly, with a halo of platinum hair and big blue eyes that turned into upside-down crescent slits every time she smiled. Which was often.

I was vibrating with nerves when I arrived at the baby gym, worried that Katie would realize I was mentally unwell and abruptly make an excuse to leave, but she immediately made me feel at home. Although I still experienced derealization when I was around her, she became one of the few people aside from Elva and my family with whom I could almost feel myself relax.

The first thing I fell in love with was Katie's voice. She sounded like a six-year-old, complete with the faintest hint of a lisp. And she soon let me know that she wasn't all Ohio-friendliness and sunshine—she had a dirty mouth and a lightning-quick mind.

As soon as we sat down, settling in next to the ball pit, Katie turned to me with a serious face. "I have a confession to make," she said. "I've been stalking you," a soft lisp on the "s" in "stalking."

I startled for a moment, wondering what she'd discovered.

"I did a deep dive into your Facebook," she said. I held my breath. "And I found out the craziest thing. You lived in freaking Morocco?!"

I exhaled a little. It turned out that she and her husband had spent time in Morocco while she had been pregnant. She had questions about my time living there, and we reminisced about the different places we had explored: the Atlas Mountain hikes, the *riads*, the souks. It felt good to get lost in remembering.

Our conversation lazily wound down various paths. We talked about motherhood, day care, work. I was still dissociating as we spoke, but I didn't have my usual urge to flee.

The babies bobbed and rolled around the gym. Nora had just started to crawl on her own, and Tommy, who was six months older, was pulling himself up, almost ready to take his first steps. We kept talking, taking breaks to feed the babies. Katie bottle fed too.

By the time we left, the light outside had already turned the deep, cool blue of an early December afternoon. We had been talking for hours.

Katie walked me halfway home. Before turning in opposite directions on the sidewalk, Katie said, "That was great. Let's do this on the reg." By the time I got home, we were already texting each other, beginning a conversation that would continue for the next four years.

Katie's husband also worked on weekends, and we began spending Saturdays or Sundays having brunch or playdates or, if it wasn't too cold, taking the babies to the park. She introduced me to other parents from day care and would sometimes invite them along on our outings. I was still quiet and reserved, but it was good for me to be out in the world, around new people. And it was good for Nora too.

Recently, I thanked Katie for being my friend when I was still so unwell, still so fragile. I thanked her for not giving up on me. "I would never give up on you," she replied. "You're a gift."

———

That winter, my life took place inside acute triangles. I went from work, to home, to therapy. From Patrick, to Elva, to Katie. Everything had to be tightly controlled. I would take pictures on the good days. Staged perfection loaded onto my phone. Posted to the highlights reel. Patrick always says that it wasn't the big events that were the hardest to live through but, rather, all the days in between.

———

Life inside the liquid suspension, the controlled confines, couldn't last forever, though. I was angry with Patrick for making me take care of Nora on my own every evening and every weekend. He was still enraged with my parents for not being there when we needed them the most. In turn, I couldn't believe how rarely his family visited or called.

Mostly, though, Patrick was furious that I had robbed him of his sense of safety within his house, within his family, within his life. He would tell me later, when the fighting began, that the slightest hitch in my voice when we spoke over the phone during his workday would make him think the worst, envision the unimaginable: that I was going to hurt myself again or, even worse, endanger Nora. He would start packing up his things, ready to clock out early and race home. Then he'd shake it off, knowing he was overreacting. Turn back to the pile of work on his desk. *Well, you shouldn't have left us alone all the time*, I would think. *You're so worried about us, but you're never here.*

213

Hell Gate Bridge

As we crept closer to Nora's first birthday, the resentments we were trying to will away by barely breathing were becoming inescapable. Their pressure created cracks in our lithosphere, fault lines patiently awaiting the inevitable quake.

Chapter Twenty-Two

For Nora's first birthday, I threw a party so beautiful, it could have been featured in one of the slick parenting magazines that had lain neatly stacked on the side table at our pediatrician's office, their glossy pages reminding me of the mother I was supposed to be.

We rented out a cavernous local smokehouse restaurant, all wood beams, big windows and mason jar glasses. I filled the space with streamers and balloons. Huge flower bouquet centerpieces. Tiered towers of cupcakes whipped high with frosting. Photographs of Nora from each month of her first year of life were suspended midair on a clothesline. Everything was pink and gold.

We invited sixty people and everyone came, filling the long wooden tables with gifts and food and pitcher after pitcher of craft beer.

Nora wore a pink tutu and tights, tiny gold ballet slippers on her feet, a white T-shirt bearing a glittering number 1, a small crown on her head.

It was Nora's day, of course, but in my mind it was also my debut. Look at how far I had come since this day last year. I was doing so well! Couldn't you tell from the lovely party I had thrown?

But I wasn't better than last year. Not much, anyway. I was still living inside my suffocating little world, closed in by sealed-shut windows and doors that never unlocked. I had just become excellent at hiding it.

All the doctors' appointments, all the medication, all my hard work at being the perfect patient, the perfect mother, the perfect wife, and nothing to show for it. It may have looked fine from the outside, but inside, twelve months later, I felt like I had barely inched forward. I was still seeing the world through the dirty glass windowpanes, still trapped in a lucid nightmare.

———

I hadn't really drank much since I had Nora. Maybe a beer or a glass of wine here and there when we got together with friends. I was so afraid of altering my reality any more than it already was, I didn't even drink coffee anymore.

At Nora's birthday celebration, someone offered me a glass of prosecco. I drank it quickly, surprising myself. The silky bubbles exploding on my tongue were delicious.

The party was open bar, and we had a generous tab. I walked over to the bar and put my empty glass down. Asked for another.

I filled up a mason jar with a syrupy IPA, another with foamy wheat beer. I accepted a glass of rosé handed to me by a friend. Soon, I no longer felt dissociated anymore. I just felt drunk. And I loved it.

———

I kept the party going all weekend. The day after Nora's birthday was Easter, and we drove down to Pennsylvania for Patrick's parents' annual celebration at their home. They had those big, two-liter bottles of Yellowtail Chardonnay packed in ice inside a cooler on the deck. I went back to the cooler all day and into the night, filling my plastic tumbler to the top, sucking down the metallic liquid until I was stumbling and numb.

I remember sitting next to my sister-in-law Leigh, who had recently separated from her boyfriend and was just beginning to navigate single motherhood. I slurred to her that I would never want to be a single mom. I didn't know how she was going to do it. All that work all alone. She stared at me, her hurt and shock at what I was saying making it impossible for her to even form a word.

Good. I thought. *Let her stare.*

———

I've always toed the line with drinking. With anything that feels good. When I was younger, it was drugs. They gave me a way to fit in and numb out. What could be better? I loved the rituals, the bonding, the late nights, the comedown. All of it.

Then everyone grew up a little and moved onto alcohol. I never realized that blacking out wasn't normal. That continuing to drink until you were sick wasn't a sign that you were having fun. But I never drank during the day, never lost a job. Never even lost my keys or my wallet. I was just having a good time.

Even now, I'm not great with things like online shopping or managing my money. Each click on the "complete purchase" button brings a rush of serotonin I have a hard time being able to live without.

But never in my life had I hit the bottom as quickly or as hard as I did during that spring and summer of 2018. I thought I was done with my free fall through hell, but it turned out there was one more nasty surprise waiting for me.

———

I started bringing home a bottle or two of wine most nights. Just a glass with dinner. Whoops! Didn't mean to fill it up so much! Maybe just one more. You know what they say: "Mommy needs wine!"

Then the bottles turned to boxes. Soon I was going through the boxes so quickly that I bought new boxes to hide in the laundry hamper in my closet. Switching them out and leveling them off to make it seem like I was still drinking the same one, even though I had thrown out the first box days ago. I hid the empties at the bottom of the recycling bin outside our apartment when I was on my way to work.

I grew ugly, inside and out. My face became bloated and red; my hair dried out to straw. My body blew up almost overnight, an extra twenty pounds settling in a layer on top of the thirty I had already gained from the medication. By late spring I weighed in at a solid 192 pounds.

But I came home from work, poured a glass of wine, and forgot all about it. I was seeing double during every bath time, and the words in the storybooks before bed were so blurry, they were barely readable. I passed out early. Woke up with my head shrieking in pain. I threw a big maxi dress over my heavy body. Showed up to work hungover with soaking wet hair.

And I got mean. I gossiped about co-workers I hardly knew. I ridiculed people's hair, clothes, and mannerisms behind their backs, cackling loudly at my own nasty jokes. I spoke poorly of my in-laws, my parents, my brothers, complaining loudly to anyone who would listen.

I bullied Patrick all the time. His job paid too little, his clothes were all wrong, he needed a haircut. Little papercuts that began to grow and fester into large, unhealable wounds.

Who. Cares. I thought. *Nothing matters, anyway. None of it.*

Prescription drugs and therapy and all my hard work hadn't done a thing. But alcohol did. And it felt *soooo* good. I had finally discovered the perfect medicine, and no one was going to take it away from me.

At first Patrick maintained his steadfast composure, even as I went completely off the rails.

"Maybe you should slow down, honey," he would say gently as I fixed myself a third vodka tonic on a Sunday afternoon. "We can have more after she goes to bed." In the early days, he drank with me at night in front of the TV or on weekends. As he grew more disgusted and afraid, he stopped.

In the beginning, if I passed out on the couch, Patrick would still stroke my hair until I awoke, the room spinning as he led me into the bedroom, his arm wrapped around my waist.

Soon, though, Patrick started to stand his ground, and every time I started hurling slurry insults in his direction, he began to hit back. The glass tank we had so carefully built around ourselves quickly shattered, the water flooding all around us.

It's either too painful or I was too drunk to remember what we said to each other. All I know was that we tore each other apart until we were unrecognizably raw. I didn't care. I kept drinking.

I began stopping into the bar for a glass of wine on my way to pick up Nora from day care. I would drink during her naps on the weekends, hungover by the time she woke up, my sunglasses on and shaking during our afternoon trips to the park. On the way home, I would stop in the liquor store to pick up a couple more bottles, Nora's stroller clumsily clanging into the overfilled shelves.

"You know how it is!" I would say cheerfully to the cashier. "Mom life!"

The cashier would smile at me with queasy concern. Then she would take my credit card and swipe it through.

If mine and Nora's safety had been on Patrick's mind while he was at work before, no matter how irrational, he now had every reason to be terrified. Even thinking about it now, I almost drop to my knees with relief that nothing terrible happened to the baby that summer. It makes me so afraid to think about what could have been that I can barely catch my breath.

It wasn't long before Patrick began threatening to leave and to take Nora with him.

"Yeah, go ahead," I would taunt him. "You wouldn't even be able to find a lawyer, let alone pay for it."

But had he gone through with it, Patrick would have had an airtight case against me. Not once during those two years did I hear the words "Children's Services." And mothers of the children I teach, mothers who live in the Queensbridge or Woodside Housing projects, mothers who don't look like me, have gotten ACS (Administration for Children's Services) called on them for far smaller infractions than psych ward stays, suicide attempts, and child neglect due to alcoholism.

Mothers of children I have taught have had agents visiting their homes because a child got a burn on their hand while helping to cook dinner, because their daughter's hair was messy, because they had a baby at home and their first grader ended up being late to school too many times. Mothers who worked so hard, who loved their children, who didn't have the time or the resources for a mental breakdown or descent into alcoholism. These were the mothers who ended up getting punished instead of me.

———

I finished the school year without fanfare. The kids had learned how to read; I didn't get fired. Summer was here.

I still saw Dr. Sarris each week, although I was dishonest about my drinking. My head was cottony and throbbing with a hangover at each of our sessions that summer.

"Just a few glasses a week," I would say. "Maybe Patrick and I have a little too much together on the weekends." I told her that I was feeling better, which in a way I was, because now I was always drunk.

In late June, Dr. Sarris told me there was a new Facebook support group for people who had DPDR and lived in the metropolitan area. "It was put together by a bunch of millennials," Dr. Sarris said, turning her palms up with a raised eyebrow and a shrug.

I found the group soon after our session and eagerly began clicking through its members. As Dr. Sarris had mentioned, most of the members were young. My heart broke for them, their lives stolen away even before they had a chance to start.

There were a few mothers in the group too. They were older than I was, in their late forties or early fifties, and their children were already young adults, but they were happy to talk to me, sharing the pain of always having a thin barrier between themselves and the people they loved the most.

After months on a waiting list, one of the younger members of the group had secured a coveted appointment with Susanna Cahalan's doctor at Lenox Hill. She stayed in the hospital for six days, monitored by an EEG for seizure activity, holding her breath the whole time, hoping for the news that the sickness inside her head was something that could be excised and thrown out.

But after six days, she didn't get the news she had been hoping for. The doctors had found abnormal activity in her brain, but they weren't able to say what they found, or how it had caused her DPDR. They told her there was a whole list of reasons as to why she could have been experiencing her dissociation, but they couldn't pinpoint anything exactly.

"They can't say why I'm fucked up, but I'm fucked up," she told me sadly. "They can only treat me symptom-wise, basically."

After the hospital stay, she was prescribed Lamictal, a seizure medication that can be effective in the treatment of dissociative disorders. She didn't take it, though.

"I feel like the go-to method is to just give us meds, but, like, what happened to us? How did this happen? Like I want to know why I'm suddenly stuck like this when I wasn't like this for twenty-four years of my life. It's like a bomb went off and I've been thrown into another dimension."

Most of my relationships with the other group members have faded, but she and I have stayed in touch. When we spoke recently, I brought up her stay at Lennox Hill, nearly three years ago, now.

"It's funny," she said ruefully. "The information I got at Lennox Hill was the last information I was given. I'm still DPDR'd as hell. I've never been able to find out what was wrong with me."

———

I spent the summer drunk and online. After Patrick and Nora left for work and day care, I would walk around the corner and buy two bottles of cheap rosé. Then, returning home, I'd park myself at the dining room table, pour myself a big, pink glass, and open my laptop.

I alternated between chatting with my friends in the DPDR Facebook group and digging through photos of my past. Anything to help me remember how happy I had once been, how pretty, how carefree. I searched for ex-boyfriends, now married homeowners with big families of their own. I fantasized what might have been had I stayed with them. I made bets that if I had, I never would have ended up like this.

Every mother misses their old life. They miss meeting up with friends, the late nights, the awful dates, the road trips. They mourn for it, especially in the early days of motherhood, when it seems as though your sense of independence has been permanently stripped. I missed those days too. And I missed the days before I became sick. What I couldn't handle, though, was that becoming a mother and becoming sick would permanently be enmeshed. How had I left so much of myself behind?

After I drained the bottles of wine, I would lie down on the couch and pass out, setting an alarm to wake myself up and wash my face before Patrick and Nora returned home from their day.

One of the afternoons in the beginning of August, I must have had too much. Maybe three bottles instead of my usual two. I slept through the alarm warning me of Patrick and Nora's arrival. I woke to Patrick shaking me with one hand, holding Nora balanced on his hip with the other.

"Hi, Mommy," Patrick said, his voice trembling.

I cracked open one eye, and then I threw up on the living room floor.

We didn't talk very much for the rest of the evening, quietly going through the routines, trying not to alarm Nora, who was growing more aware of the world by the day.

After Nora was in bed, Patrick and I sat down on the couch, facing each other. He was exhausted, weak with defeat. That night, he was too worn down for a fight.

"You always talk about how much you wish you had been more present when she was an infant," he started. "You always look at pictures, saying how you wish more than anything that you could get that time back. Now you're not totally better, but you have the chance to be more present. To be here for your little girl. And now you're going to miss this part too."

"And if I don't stop?" I asked.

"Then that's it. I take Nora to my parent's house. I can't do this anymore. We're done."

We stared at each other across the gulf between us, tears streaming down our faces, saying nothing. There was nothing more we needed to say.

———

Next door to our apartment was a VFW. Each night, the VFW hosted a meeting. And each night, after Nora went to sleep, I went next door, sat down on a metal folding chair, and I listened.

———

During the summer of 2018, Nora hit her major milestones. She took her first steps, she said "Dada" and "Memmy." She gave kisses. She started to say, "I yuv you." I drank through all of it.

For all the humiliations I suffered during those two years, there is no shame that burns more ferociously for me than the months that I drank. I deleted every single photograph from that time. Even now, I still don't have the courage to stand face-to-face with the wreckage.

———

After I stopped drinking, it was as if Patrick and I had emerged from a long spell inside a fallout shelter. We surveyed the rubble of the world before us, disoriented and unsure of where to go next. But we were still whole. We had remained intact.

Patrick and I had a lot of work to do to repair all that had been broken and lost. We still do. Our fights are louder. We're better at knowing how to slice each other down with a single sharp word. Patrick's obsession with my and Nora's safety hasn't diminished but rather continues to grow, hanging so heavy over our heads that at times it nearly debilitates us.

I blame myself. I still haven't let go of the guilt. I haven't let go of the shame. Neither of us has let go of the anger at the hand we were dealt, and it's that ugly black seed of anger that still causes us to drift. But we make our way back.

Chapter Twenty-Three

As summer flowed into fall and I headed back to work, my disorder began to shape-shift again. There were no more dirty glass panes or suffocating boxes. From those confines, I had been freed. Instead, I felt like I was constantly glitching. My world became like a record that played smoothly, and then, suddenly, the needle would skip, bumping awkwardly across the tracks. Still, I found it preferable to feeling imprisoned.

As the days passed, there were longer stretches when I could almost see the world clearly. I could talk to more people outside my tight circle. I laughed more often. I even started being able to make other people laugh again too. Then the glitching would start, the tape would fast-forward, pause, rewind, and I would have to begin all over.

I was always asking Elva if I seemed better yet. She told me to be patient. Not quite yet, but she saw it coming.

Recently, when I asked her to recall our second year at work together, she told me that in the fall of 2018, I still wasn't quite the same person she had once known. That there were days I was fine and there were days when she could see my brain running in circles, days when she could see that I was having, as she called it, one of my "outer body" experiences. Even so, that fall, she saw more signs of life in me, more promises that I might return.

Elva was pregnant again, this time with a baby girl. She already knew her daughter's name: She would call her Emma.

Elva was excited, but, unlike her previous pregnancy, this one was much less smooth. She was constantly sick and exhausted, and feeling far more fragile than she had when she was pregnant with Robert, her son. She was quicker to snap at the kids, at me, on the phone with her mom or husband. She was also going to school at night and on the weekends. Always just one step ahead of breaking down. I understood. I picked up the slack she had given to me last year and tried to let her rest.

Still, we had fun. Elva and I loved celebrity gossip, and she came into the classroom each morning before the kids arrived with her Dunkin' egg sandwich and chocolate doughnut, prepared to spill. We would sit down at our little desk, and as she ate her breakfast, she would relay the news she had heard on the local pop radio station during her drive to work.

That fall, the biggest news on the celebrity front was the love story of pop star Ariana Grande and comedian Pete Davidson. From Patrick's aunts in Oxford, Pennsylvania, to my first graders, I didn't know anyone who wasn't following the scoop.

Like most people over forty, before the celebrity romance was blasted over every news outlet in America, I hadn't really paid very much attention to Pete Davidson. But I did now.

I paid attention to how openly he spoke about his struggles with mental illness. I paid attention to how he normalized it. He repeated the message that I wanted to share with the world but had been too afraid to: Mental illnesses are chronic and common and should be treated as such. And he made his struggles accessible, hilariously riffing on his mental health on *SNL*'s "Weekend Update" or posting touching messages on Instagram to raise awareness, ending the posts with the words "I see you. I hear you."

Like my friend Sam from New York East, Pete Davidson had been diagnosed with borderline personality disorder. They fit the profile perfectly—their charisma and sense of humor so palpable, they could practically set a room on fire. Yet no one knew that behind that bright facade, the seductive whisper of suicide beckons those who suffer from BPD into the darkness.

Similar to DPDR or agitated depression, borderline personality disorder is also frequently misdiagnosed as bipolar disorder. Doctors can have patients on the wrong medications for a long time, often to detrimental effect. Also like DPDR, borderline personality disorder can take years to be correctly identified. In a 2017 clip on *SNL*, Pete Davidson shares his relief at finally having received the diagnosis he had been searching for. He got his label, his box.

I began to pay attention to how the dialogue around mental illness was slowly shifting, especially within the Gen Z community. Young people seemed to share more openly and passionately about their own struggles and how they were working to advocate for change. Terms like "holding space" and "making yourself vulnerable" started to appear in the conversation. The arms were opening, ushering in acceptance. *I see you. I hear you.*

The following fall, when I started teaching middle school, I was floored at how open my students were when talking about mental health. They spoke with one another about anxiety and depression and questioning gender identity with the passion I usually reserved for talking to my middle school friends about my favorite member of New Kids on the Block. They would casually bow out of after-school plans, letting their friends know they couldn't hang out because they had a therapy appointment. I loved it. It gives me hope that Nora will grow up in a world where she will never have to feel as though she's an outsider, where she will never have to feel isolated and alone.

I also noticed that the conversation around the topic of pregnancy had started changing too. It was becoming more honest, more raw. The comedian Ali Wong had a stand-up special where she spoke openly about her miscarriage. Amy Schumer created a docuseries where she chronicled her difficult pregnancy, step by step. More women began opening up about postpartum depression and anxiety. The image of the beaming, all-natural earth mother was becoming replaced with a more realistic portrait.

I started to take it easier on myself as a mother. I deleted all the mommy-influencer accounts I followed; I logged out of the Facebook message boards. I stopped worrying so much that Nora wasn't consuming organic vegetable purées and that her tastes tended more toward dinosaur shaped chicken nuggets and string cheese. I let her play with plastic Disney Princess dolls because she loved them. I no longer berated myself because she didn't own any organic toys—I still don't even really know what organic toys are. And I stopped feeling so guilty about not having breastfed. If I am honest with myself, I don't think I would have done it for very long anyway.

Nora was healthy and loving and bright. She was thriving. I must have been doing something right. I still have times when I doubt myself. As a sister, as a friend. As a wife. But I rarely doubt myself as a mother anymore. Nora doesn't let me.

———

The fall rolled on, and the stretches of clarity beginning to outnumber the periods of dissociation. By the time December approached, the clarity was winning out.

There were still times when I dissociated. Transitions were always difficult—going from work to home, or the first moments of entering a social gathering—before I settled in. Bright lights and crowded places still brought on feelings of unreality. Even now, if I find myself walking down Steinway Street, I need to look down at the sidewalk and count my breaths.

When I'm anxious, I still skip over sweaty palms or palpable heartbeats and go straight to derealization, floating outside of my body and into the lucid dream. But now I return. I can always return.

It was as though I had spent the last two years trapped within a wall of sound, turned up to the highest decibel. And then the reverberations. And, finally, silence.

I wish there was a more dramatic or precise way to describe my recovery. A magic pill or word or treatment that had brought me back into the world, back into myself. An otherworldly harbinger of hope that crossed my path, letting me know that my years of suffering were coming to an end. But really, it was just time. Hard work and the long passage of time.

I think about Dr. Simeon's unrelenting insistence on exposure therapy. In Andrew Solomon's book *Far from the Tree*, in the chapter on schizophrenia, he cites the law professor Elyn Saks, who lives with the disorder. Saks is a proponent for treating mental illness with psychoanalysis and behavioral therapy, likening it to how speech and physical therapy might help a stroke victim learn to talk again or walk again. She advocates that with psychoanalysis and behavioral therapy, a patient can slowly train and strengthen their mind. Medication helped clear my anxiety and depression, but I think more than anything, it was Dr. Simeon's emphasis on behavioral therapy that enabled me to live again.

And I think about the doctors' predictions that I would get well because my illness occurred within the context of my pregnancy. How Dr. Klein said that if she saw me on the street in five years, I would no longer be on lithium. About that, she was right. Maybe there is something to the idea that mental illnesses that occur during pregnancy and the postpartum period more easily remit. Women who experience postpartum psychosis do not generally go on to have lifelong schizoaffective disorders, and women who experience postpartum depression usually recover fairly quickly with treatment. Maybe this is what happened to me.

I do know that out of the three or four women I keep in touch with from the DPDR group, I am the only one whose symptoms have remitted. *How?* They always ask. *How did you do it?* I always joke, trying to smile through the pain behind their questions. *I think having a toddler has shocked me back into reality*, I say. We laugh. *Maybe I should get knocked up*, they always reply. We laugh again, sadly. We try to move on.

———

Even though I was feeling better, things between Patrick and me were still fragile. Like two magnets of the same poles, we orbited around each other, never touching, pushing each other away. We had forgotten how to be together outside of the crisis mode, how to function without holding our breath.

I brought up our relationship struggles in my sessions with Dr. Sarris. She had a simple solution to the problem: date nights. I demurred.

Babysitters were $20 an hour, and that on top of dinner would end up being almost $200 for a night out. She shrugged. "Takeout and Netflix on the couch then," she said. "I don't think it's the money; I think you're afraid."

She was right. I was afraid to be alone with Patrick again. We spoke through Nora now, crowing over her achievements and milestones. Reminding each other to write the check for day care, to schedule her checkups, or checking in to see whose night it was to read bedtime stories. I was afraid that if Patrick and I were alone together, we would discover that our relationship couldn't be saved or, worse, that there was nothing worth saving.

We hadn't been on a date since Nora was born. It was another part of parenting that we still hadn't learned. For our first date, we had one of Nora's teachers from her day care come over to babysit. We worried she would cry when we left, but Nora was so excited to have her beloved day-care teacher Mrs. Violeta in our home that she didn't even look up when we said goodbye.

Patrick and I went to a local restaurant that served comfort food like mac and cheese and burgers. The atmosphere was low-lit and intimate, perfect for an early December night. I wore a dress and boots and blow-dried my hair straight. I put on red lipstick. We were nervous.

At the restaurant, we sat across from each other, but the table was small and we could lean in close to talk. We were shy, talking about safe subjects like work, but it didn't feel forced, and the restaurant felt safe and warm.

Outside, after dinner, we kissed on the sidewalk and held hands on the walk home. When we got back to the apartment, Nora was sound asleep in her crib. Mrs. Violeta sat reading on our couch. "The baby was perfect," she said.

Dr. Sarris checked in every week to make certain I was completing my homework assignments. In each session, I was to describe the date,

233

what we had talked about, and how I had felt. We continued this routine until she felt that Patrick and I had begun to heal. Eventually, she didn't bring it up anymore.

The dates weren't always a babysitter and dinner. As I had told Dr. Sarris, those were expensive evenings and we were still getting back on our feet, paying off the medical bills we continued to receive. More often, our dates were ordering in from a favorite restaurant and having dinner together after Nora went to bed, then watching a movie on the couch, each week leaning into each other more closely.

We had skipped over our second anniversary, staying home with Nora, but for our third wedding anniversary, we planned for a night out. To Nora's delight, Mrs. Violeta came back and shooed us out the door as quickly as she arrived.

We had dinner reservations at a beautiful local trattoria, and on the walk over we admired the over-the-top Christmas decorations that lit the neighborhood homes, still up before the New Year arrived.

Like at our first anniversary dinner at Del Posto, we talked about music and friends and reminisced about our wedding, but this time, instead of pretending, I was actually clear. We kept talking long after the dessert plates were cleared away.

After dinner, we took a picture together outside the restaurant. The picture looks similar to the one we took on our first anniversary. My bangs are dark and shiny and my face is flushed. But this time my face is flushed with joy. My eyes are focused, and my smile is real. I look at this picture all the time. It reminds me of when I started to return to myself—and when Patrick and I started to return to each other.

Chapter Twenty-Four

Nora's birthdays are how I mark time now, and for me, March is when the year renews. The start of spring.

As Nora's birthday approached, I started getting rid of things, replacing items in the house with something new. Anything dark was gone. I only wanted whites and soft grays, rice-paper lamps that glowed in low light, hanging plants. I switched out all the photos in the picture frames, putting the old ones in a dresser drawer. I only wanted reminders of the more recent times, to store away the times from before until I was ready to revisit them.

I threw out my old clothes from the first year, even socks and underwear, shoving them in big black trash bags and leaving them on the curb the night before garbage pickup. If I could have, I would have burned them. Nora's clothes got packed in plastic boxes and were stored in our hallway.

I threw out Nora's mobile, the one that had hung over her bassinette and twinkled out the notes to Elvis Presley's "Teddy Bear" during an early March snowstorm, the flakes sticking to my eyelashes and blurring my vision as I shoved the bag in the trash can. I could hear the last notes through the can's metal lid, growing mournful and slow as the battery ran out.

———

Elva left for her maternity leave and gave birth to Emma on March 15th—two weeks before Nora's second birthday.

"I knew you were better," she told me, "because I didn't feel bad leaving you. I knew you were going to be okay on your own."

———

That March, within a few weeks of each other, Patrick and I both got new jobs. Patrick would still work in the art world, but this time his schedule was a regular 9 to 6. And, finally, we were all home together on the weekends.

For me, I wouldn't begin until the following fall, but I had been offered a job as the English Language Arts teacher at the middle school. Richard knew that my major passion was reading, and when he heard about the job opening, he passed it along. It would be a big jump from early elementary, where I had been for more than a decade, but we both knew that I was ready for a change.

We held Nora's second birthday at our home, just our closest friends and family this time. We ordered six-foot Godfather hoagies and had chips and soda and juice boxes. My mother ordered a sheet cake decorated with a picture of a white cat wearing black cat-eye glasses. This year we didn't serve alcohol—not on purpose; we just weren't really thinking about it.

Both sets of grandparents came—Nora's favorite people. Patrick and I ache with tenderness when we watch her with her Grandmas and her Grandpa and PopPop. Their love is so pure. They don't expect anything from one another.

Dr. Sarris thinks that it's healing for me to see my parents and Nora together. I think so too. Anything they couldn't give to me, they give to Nora. Their love for her is unbidden.

The photograph that was taken of Nora blowing out the candles on her kitten cake is one I always come back to. At two years old, Nora is so lovely she can take a stranger's breath away. Her blonde hair curls softly around her head, and her blue eyes are so long lashed, they look as if they are framed by feather hand fans. She's ethereal.

In the picture, Nora's cheesing hard, her fork already stuck in the cake, ready to dig in. Patrick and I are crouched on either side of her highchair. We're grinning widely too. I'm still heavy in the photo, but I'd started to own it, feeling good in my clothes again, and in my skin. Patrick is handsome in his glasses and flannel, his face a blissed-out daze, like he can't believe his luck.

When I look at that photograph, Nora about to make her second-birthday wish, my heart starts to quicken with the reminder of how happy we were—how happy we are—that I'd finally returned, that I'd come back to our family.

———

The school year ended sweetly. My students gave a presentation on animal habitats and sang "Seasons of Love" from *Rent*, with edited lyrics. They were proud of themselves. I was proud too. I would miss teaching the younger students, but I was excited for my new position.

I would see them in four years, anyway, when they were middle schoolers, slouching and surly as they sat through my ELA class.

———

That summer, I worked on getting my body healthy again. Although I had stopped drinking, I held onto the weight. Each morning, I headed to the gym. I came home, made lunch, took walks around the neighborhood. And I read. My deepest pleasure, which I was unable to enjoy when I was sick, my mind unable to comprehend any written words. I started with all the books I had missed in 2017 and worked my way forward.

A few days a week, I kept Nora home from day care and took her to the parks with sprinklers or to the Museum of Television and Radio, only a few blocks from our home. They had a long-standing exhibition of the Muppets.

Our favorite thing to do together, though, was taking the long walk to Astoria Park and using their public swimming pool. The locker rooms and pool were crowded and dingy—both of us came down with ear infections, pink eye, and athlete's foot from our visits. But we loved it. Nora was fearless in the water. She would dunk her face under and then come back up laughing, shaking her head and crowing, "I'm a doggie shaking; I'm a doggie!" She liked to pretend she was a baby sea lion and would lie flat on her belly on top of my back, holding my shoulders as I swam breaststrokes through the lukewarm water. We stayed in the pool for hours, Nora refusing to get out until the pads of her fingers shriveled like prunes.

The pool was in the center of Astoria Park, in the hollow of a hill, surrounded by tall, leafy trees. In the distance, to the left, was the Queensboro Bridge. To the right was the Hell Gate. I barely noticed it. It didn't mean anything to me anymore. It was just a bridge.

On a whim, I looked up the history of the Hell Gate Bridge, wondering where its ominous name had originated. It turns out it has nothing to do with the Gates of Hell after all. It's from the word *Hellgat*, a Dutch word meaning "clear passage."

———

When it was time to go back to school in late August, I was finally ready for my big return. I had lost weight and bought new clothes. I was feeling good about myself. And I was excited to start my new job. I set up my new classroom to be soothing and calm, all watercolors and plants and Himalayan salt lamps. I hung framed posters with quotes from young adult books, including one from *Coraline* by Neil Gaiman, the novel we would be beginning the year with. It was my favorite quote from the book, when The Cat tells Coraline to "Be Wise. Be Brave. Be Tricky."

I had always liked teaching well enough, but I loved teaching middle school. My students were willing and open. I was surprised at how excited they were to learn, to be there with me.

I hammed it up, fully owning the role of the English teacher, with my glasses hooked onto my cardigan, holding onto a cup of coffee as I perched on the edge of a desk, reading aloud from my favorite passages. I loved listening to the kids make connections to the books and to their world and the world around them. One of my students that fall said he felt that Neil Gaiman was an artist, that instead of creating art with paint and a canvas, he used his words and the page.

I worked with a new team of teachers. They were more serious than my elementary school friends. We didn't talk about celebrity gossip or diets, and they didn't have kids, so they weren't too interested in hearing about parenting. We talked a lot about the news or movies. We talked about our work. We were all excited to be doing what we were doing.

Even though my new team was more serious about their work, we still laughed all the time, especially when talking about the kids, and reminiscing about our own preadolescent selves. The four of us grew close quickly.

At home, things were going well too. No matter what my size, Patrick has always found a way to let me know that he thinks I am beautiful. Still, that fall, with my newly healthy body and my happy state of mind, he seemed more attracted to me than ever. Even with two full-time jobs and a toddler, we were having sex almost as often as we had that Brooklyn summer on the fire escape.

We were careful—sort of—using a loose rhythm method where we didn't have sex when I was ovulating. I figured that at age forty-one, I probably wasn't going to get pregnant that easily anyway.

One Saturday morning that fall, we were getting ready for a trip out to Corona to visit the Queens Hall of Science when I realized that it had been a while since I'd gotten my period. I had an ancient pregnancy test lying in the cabinet beneath our bathroom sink. Impulsively, I took the test, and almost immediately the second pink line appeared.

There was no way I was pregnant, was there? I jogged across the street to CVS to buy a fresh pack and came home to try again. And again. The answer blinked up at me from the plastic stick in block letters: "PREGNANT."

Patrick and I still managed to get through the day at the museum, calm despite the news hanging over us. That evening, we sat on the couch, quiet, knowing what we had to do.

I was on four different medications now—two of which I wouldn't be able to take during pregnancy; one that, if I was trying to get pregnant, I should have gone off months before. It wouldn't be fair to any of us for me to take that risk of trying. Not to me, not to Patrick, and especially not to Nora. She needed her mom.

Still, we were heartbroken. When we daydreamed about what it would be like to have another, even though we knew we couldn't, it was always a girl. We had even picked out a name: Natalie. Even so, we remained clear on our decision. We could only have one child. She would be Nora. And she would be enough. We made an appointment at Planned Parenthood for the following weekend.

———

My mom came to our apartment to watch Nora the day of our appointment. She never wavered in her support of our choice, never made us feel like it was the wrong thing to do.

In the car on the way to Brooklyn Heights, we were quiet. I had never been to a Planned Parenthood and had no idea what to expect. When we walked through the doors, it looked like I had imagined, which was not unlike the DMV. But the care I received there was nothing like I had imagined at all.

The procedure itself only took a few minutes, but the process to help me get through it took hours. I was never kept waiting, though I moved from physical exams to meetings with doctors, counselors, and social workers as the all-female staff gently guided me through each step, taking their time, making sure I was comfortable, informing me so that I wouldn't need to feel afraid.

During the actual procedure and afterward, I had a doula. She held my hand and coached me through breathing exercises, reminding me to focus on her words, on her face. When it was over, she wheeled me into the recovery room and waited patiently with me until I was ready to go home.

The stark contrast between the care I received for those few hours at Planned Parenthood and at the Labor and Delivery ward where I gave birth to Nora hit me like a sucker punch.

No one prepares you for childbirth. Ask any mother and she will tell you the same, that a not-so-small part of you believes that when you walk into the hospital, it will be like the movies: Your water will break, soaking the back seat of the cab as the driver weaves through traffic at breakneck speed, honking horns blaring into the late city night. You will be immediately rushed into a private room by a young, wide-eyed attendant who is just as thrilled as you are. In the room, your doctor will be waiting, masked up in full green scrubs. You will sit up on your hospital bed with your bent legs spread open, chewing ice cubes, slathering on lip balm, cursing at your partner, who will calmly brush the sweaty hair from your forehead.

Suddenly, it will be time to push. You will squeeze nearby hands, your face twisting into a grimace, clenching your teeth and you will *push*! Maybe you have to try a few times. Then you will groan, and out comes the head. A few plaintive wails before your partner proudly cuts the cord. Your baby at your naked breast, all clean and new smelling, a snug little cap on their head. You weep, your partner weeps, the nurses weep. Your beautiful new family.

I always used to tell my pregnant friends who asked about my birthing experience not to listen to me, that my pregnancy and childbirth were very far from the norm. But as I collected more stories, stories from mothers who had pregnancies that were easy and smooth, I learned that most of them, like me, ended up being totally blindsided by their birthing experience.

Here's what no one tells you: In labor or not, you will be lying in that hospital bed for at least eighteen hours, usually closer to thirty-six. If you are getting induced, you will be given the epidural the moment you walk in, so that when it comes time to push, about a day later, the epidural will have completely worn off. You will be hooked up to every monitor ever designed for use in a hospital, which makes it incredibly difficult to adjust your position on the bed you will lie on for a day or more. Still, you will be encouraged to sleep, to rest, by any hospital employee who walks into your room. And there will be many. Pee will flow down your leg into a bag through the catheter that has been inserted inside you. The bag will fill up often, because the only thing you can ingest is liquids: broth, juice, maybe Jell-O if you're lucky. You won't be sure why the teacher at the hospital-provided birthing class told you to be sure to pack healthy snacks, like you're going on a class trip. Then again, she told you that if you are in pain, to remember to "breathe through your vagina." Nurses will cycle in and out as their shifts end and begin. Residents come by and make notes on a clipboard. Your doctor will be nowhere in sight. They don't show up until you become dilated, about twelve hours later.

Although Patrick and I were clear on the decision we had made, we still mourned the loss. And after our experience with the women who cared for me at Planned Parenthood, we mourned the loss of the care we should have had during my pregnancy and Nora's birth but never did.

When the procedure was over, we returned home to Nora and my mother. It was late afternoon and I was woozy, and tired. My mother left, and Patrick made a simple dinner. After we put Nora to bed, we fell asleep soon after, tangled up like we used to. We were always trying to heal, always healing.

Patrick and I got better, closer, and I slowly started to gain more confidence as a mom. I told everyone that at age forty-one, I had finally found my dream job. That winter, I think, was the happiest I have ever been. I would tell people that when they asked how I was doing. "I'm happy," I said. And I meant it.

Chapter Twenty-Five

As Nora's birthday approached that year, though, the world closed and we were shuttered in, the three of us bewildered and afraid inside our apartment. We scanned the news from morning until night, trying to glean any information we could until we stopped completely, realizing that no one knew any more than we did. We lived only two miles from Elmhurst Hospital, and sirens wailed, the flashing red lights glowing on our bedroom walls. We were unable to sleep.

School shut down, and we scrambled. I tried to figure out how to teach online, to figure out how to convince my students that they were safe in a world they no longer recognized. They cried. Most of them lived in East Elmhurst, ground zero. Their parents got sick. They lost grandparents, aunts, uncles. Some of them got sick too.

Nora's third birthday passed. I still decorated the whole house and ordered her a sparkly dress. This year she was old enough to understand that it was her birthday, and how it was supposed to have been celebrated. She wondered where her friends were and why they couldn't come. She asked me if they had "flown away." We ate a chocolate cake topped with buttercream frosting and dotted with rainbow sprinkles. We blew out the candles with our friends and family over Zoom.

Dr. Sarris was worried about me; she thought that being in a crisis mode might make me relapse into anxiety or depression, or worse. I was okay, though. It didn't come back.

I used all the remedies that had been prescribed to make me feel better before: the bubble baths, the Sun Salutations. I drank tea. I talked on the phone with my friends and my family for hours, reconnecting with Zach and Celine, who were living a parallel life with their young daughters across the ocean. When it got warmer, I took walks. I noticed all the rose bushes that people tended to in their yards. I realized that Queens was kind of beautiful. This time, the remedies worked fine. I was able to be a caretaker. I didn't need much taking care of anymore.

Nora was a mess—isolated and stir-crazy. I ran through every early childhood activity I could think of, trying to keep her steady. Patrick and I juggled trying to get work done with keeping her happy. We were snappy, with her, with each other. At the end of the day, the three of us flopped onto the couch in a pile, completely spent.

I ordered art supplies, dress-up clothes, books, shovels and pails, box after box delivered to our stoop. None of it held Nora's attention. The only thing she was interested in was sitting in a roasting pan filled with dish soap bubbles and food coloring. She ran through the house wet and naked, her bottom permanently dyed blue. Eventually she stopped putting on clothes completely and started streaking through my online classes wearing only a crown.

We were exhausted and frightened, but as we settled into the new, bizarre realities of our routines, an odd sense of contentment fell over our home.

I began waking up at dawn to take long walks, through Astoria Park and down to the East River. On the walks, I started coming up with a theory about love. I thought about the feeling of being in love, that sweet melt in your belly, that bubble caught between your throat and your chest. I thought about how no matter who you felt it toward, it was always the same. Nora's breath on my neck when she climbed into our bed in the morning. My student's understanding that writing was painting with words. My fingers interlaced with Patrick's on the fire escape. It was all the same feeling.

———

In early June we started a new routine to help bring a softer ending to the long days. After dinner, Patrick chose a record, put it on the Victrola, and we tucked in the dining room chairs and we danced.

One night, Patrick chose our favorite record, Kacey Musgraves's *Golden Hour.* Each one of us, even Nora, knew almost all the words to every song. When anyone asked Nora what her favorite song was, instead of answering "Twinkle, Twinkle, Little Star" or "The Wheels on the Bus," Nora would chirp, "Kacey!" in her little sparrow voice.

That night, we had the windows in the dining room open. It was one of those in-between evenings, where it was too warm in the house but not quite warm enough to turn on the air conditioner.

I was holding Nora in my arms, her string-bean legs wrapped around my waist, her sweaty chest spongy against mine. She was wearing nothing but a tutu and a crown.

The song "Golden Hour" came on, the song I always say is my song for Nora. I wish there was a deeper reason, but really it's because it makes me think of Nora's golden hair, or the way she glows. Still, I love the lyrics. That night, I sang into her blonde curls as Patrick danced next to us, shuffling along in his flip-flops.

We were hot; we were exhausted. We knew that coming next were the struggles of bath time, the endless princess stories before bed. The anxiety of the evening news. But for those few moments, as I swayed Nora back and forth on my hip, we were held close, suspended in the honey light that slipped in through the wooden slats of the window shades. We were happy. We were together. We were home.

Acknowledgments

This book would not exist without Sarah Perry, the best mentor, writer and friend. Thank you for believing in my story and for believing in me. You have my utmost gratitude.

Thank you to the fiercest, kindest, most brilliant agent, JL Stermer. I can't believe how lucky I am to have you in my corner. And thank you to Kari Boston for the introduction! I'm so lucky to have you in my corner, too.

Thank you to Miranda Heyman, David LeGere and the rest of the team at Woodhall for the opportunity to publish with you–it's been nothing but joy since day one.

I am also completely indebted to Molly Brouillette Ellis for all your help with marketing, publicity, and so much more.

Thank you, Elizabeth Ellen, for your mentorship and more importantly, your friendship. Your generosity astounds me. Thank you also to all the writers who offered support and advice along the way: Elle Nash, Chelsea Bieker, Chloe Caldwell, Mila Jaroniec, Allie Rowbottom, Kate Brody, Kailey DelloRusso. What a coven! The sisterhood of women writers is a powerful one.

To my earliest readers and most beloved friends, Sara Cardillo, Katie Berkshire McNulty, Andrea Tighe and Bryan Quinn, thank you for cheering me on, supporting me and most of all, for making life so loving and fun.

To my AoC family, especially Richard Lee and Elva Incantalupo, I would quite literally not have survived without you. Thank you for providing me with the care and understanding I needed to heal.

To Dr. S.–It's been a long and often painful journey but look where we are now. Words can't express our gratitude to you.

To Zach Miskin and Celine Poulfort, I love you. Thank you for never letting me go throughout the worst parts. Zach, my earliest reader, thank you for convincing me to keep going.

To Alex Miskin, thank you for your gentle kindness and your love. Always my baby brother.

Solomon and Michelle Miskin, the most supportive and loving parents and grandparents. I don't even know where to begin. Thank you for giving me everything. I love you.

Thank you to Tom and Ida McIntyre for being in-law and grandparents extraordinaire and for raising an incredible son. And to Leigh McIntyre, the best aunt this side of the Atlantic, I'm so lucky to have you as my "sister".

To Patrick McIntyre, everything I am, everything I have, is because of you. I wake up each day so happy because I know I get to spend it by your side. Even on the bad days. You are my partner in all ways and the love of my life.

And to Nora. My light. How lucky I am to love you.

About the Author

Barrie Miskin, a survivor of a severe and rare maternal mental illness, writes from a personal lens on maternal and mental health. Her essays, creative nonfiction and interviews have appeared in Hobart, Narratively, Motherwell, Write or Die Magazine and elsewhere. She is a fellowship recipient from The Cullman Center Institute for Teachers as well as the Unruly Retreat for Writers. Barrie lives in Queens, New York with her husband and daughter.